Learning to Hide:
The English Learning Classroom as Sanctuary and Trap

A Volume in:
Education Policy in Practice: Critical Cultural Studies

Series Editors:
Rodney Hopson
Edmund Hamann

Education Policy in Practice: Critical Cultural Studies

Series Editors:

Rodney Hopson
University of Illinois

Edmund Hamann
University of Nebraska-Lincoln

Series Books

Paths to the Future of Higher Education (2021)
Brian L. Foster, Steven W. Graham, & Joe F. Donaldson

*Navigating the Volatility of Higher Education:
Anthropological and Policy Perspectives* (2018)
Brian L. Foster, Steven W. Graham, & Joe F. Donaldson

Revisiting Education in the New Latino Diaspora (2015)
Edmund Hamann, Stanton Wortham, & Enrique G. Murillo Jr.

*The Construction, Negotiation, and Representation of Immigrant
Student Identities in South African schools* (2015)
Saloshna Vandeyar & Thirusellvan Vandeyar

Researching Race in Education: Policy, Practice and Qualitative Research (2014)
Adrienne D. Dixon

Educated for Change? Muslim Refugee Women in the West (2012)
Patricia Buck & Rachel Silver

*Placing Practitioner Knowledge at the Center of Teacher Education:
Rethinking the Policies and Practices of the Education Doctorate* (2012)
Margaret Macintyre Latta & Susan Wunder

Hopes in Friction: Schooling, Health and Everyday Life in Uganda (2009)
Lotte Meinert

*War or Common Cause? A Critical Ethnography of Language Education
Policy, Race, and Cultural Citizenship* (2009)
Kimberly Anderson

*Advancing Democracy Through Education?
U.S. Influence Abroad and Domestic Practices* (2008)
Doyle Stevick & Bradley A. U. Levinson

Civil Sociality: Children, Sport, and Cultural Policy in Denmark (2008)
Sally Anderson

*Challenging the System? A Dramatic Tale of
Neoliberal Reform in an Australian High School* (2006)
Martin Forsey

*Tend the Olive, Water the Vine: Globalization and the
Negotiation of Early Childhood in Palestine* (2006)
Rachel Christina

*Schooled for the Future? Educational Policy and
Everyday Life among Urban Squatters in Nepal* (2006)
Karen Valentin

Civil Society or Shadow State? State/NGO Relations in Education (2004)
Margaret Sutton & Robert F. Arnove

Learning to Hide:
The English Learning Classroom as Sanctuary and Trap

Tricia Hagen Gray

INFORMATION AGE PUBLISHING, INC.
Charlotte, NC • www.infoagepub.com

Library of Congress Cataloging-In-Publication Data

The CIP data for this book can be found on the Library of Congress website (loc.gov).

Paperback: 979-8-88730-565-3
Hardcover: 979-8-88730-566-0
E-Book: 979-8-88730-567-7

Copyright © 2024 Information Age Publishing Inc.

All rights reserved. No part of this publication may be reproduced, stored in a retrieval system, or transmitted, in any form or by any means, electronic, mechanical, photocopying, microfilming, recording or otherwise, without written permission from the publisher.

Printed in the United States of America

CONTENTS

Acknowledgements vii

Preface ix

Introduction: Mayberry in Flux xv

1. The Political Work of the ELL Program at WRHS 1

2. The People in the Classroom 13

3. Constructing Sanctuary 29

4. Mismatch 45

5. The Implications of Care 55

6. Missed Opportunities in the Classroom and School 77

7. The Paradoxical Tensions of Sanctuary and Trap 87

8. "Hear Us, See Us" 101

References 109

Author Biography 129

ACKNOWLEDGEMENTS

I entered this work with the hope of illuminating the realities of young newcomers to the United States to inform more equitable experiences of school and citizenship. I am profoundly grateful to Mrs. Durham, Mrs. Sánchez, Isabel, Caterín Michelle, Anyelín, Saraí, Sayra, Jesús, and Alejandro and all the students in this classroom at WRHS for allowing me to tell their stories and trusting that I would do so with care. I am grateful to have had the support of a core group of passionate, thoughtful, and justice-oriented scholars for this project and beyond: Drs. Lauren Gatti, Edmund "Ted" Hamann, Jenelle Reeves, Loukia Sarroub, and Wayne Babchuk, thank you. Dr. Aprille Phillips, dear friend and colleague, you make me remember *why this matters*. Dr. Aaron Musson, your feedback from our office conversations is most certainly reflected in these pages. Dr. Mardi Schmeichel, your endless support and mentorship make all the Dr. Pepper trips worth it. My heartfelt thanks to my former students and colleagues at Cass Lake-Bena High School (including the KAC!) who are forever a part of me; this work is in many ways a testament to what I learned there. Tony, thanks for your partnership and faith in me; Boone and Lily, you make me proud to be your mom and you help me remember why I do this work; Sota, thanks for the companionship that only an old dog could offer while I wrote the majority of these pages, and Auggie, thanks for the bright spot you are in our family and for keeping my lap warm as I finished this manuscript. To all my family, your love and support make me brave enough to do this work.

PREFACE

The stillness of shock weighed heavily on the morning of November 9, 2016. The public, many exhausted from late nights watching returns, had just learned the results of the U.S. Presidential election the previous night. Women all over the country had worn white to the voting booth on November 8 in a nod to the suffragettes of the early 1900s who worked to claim women's right to vote, and in this election, a woman—Hillary Rodham Clinton—was poised to be the next President of the United States. With polling showing a slim but consistent lead, her election seemed inevitable after the contentious and polarizing campaigns both she and her opponent, Donald Trump, had run. As election results were publicized on the evening of November 8, concern and bewilderment over the unlikely result intensified. Almost impossibly, it seemed, Donald Trump would be our country's next President.

For many, including me, the feeling was distinctly dystopian, much like the numbness I recall experiencing throughout the day of September 11, 2001, and in the days following. On this November morning, I wondered who we were as a country and questioned the progress we had made in the name of civil and human rights. The ugliness of the Trump campaign—the misogyny, sexism, racism, white nationalism, and nativism so blatantly on display—had been divisive, to say the least. His personal and professional history, at several passes during his campaign, seemed to preclude and disqualify him from holding the highest office

Learning to Hide: The English Learning Classroom as Sanctuary and Trap
pages ix–xiv.
Copyright © 2024 by Information Age Publishing
www.infoagepub.com
All rights of reproduction in any form reserved.

in the nation (see, for example, Keith Olbermann recount the list of "176 Reasons Donald Trump Should Not Be President Using Trump's Own Words" [Olbermann, 2016]). While it's impossible to identify the most egregious offenses, certainly many thought he would not be able to survive as a legitimate choice for President of the United States especially after the release of a recording in which Trump boasts of his ability to sexually assault women with no repercussions—which he later dismissed as "locker room talk" (Fahrenthold, 2016).

The groups Trump offended during his 2016 campaign span the spectrum of all identity descriptors. However, perhaps most outrageous was Trump's campaign promise to build a wall on the southern border the United States shares with Mexico. His assault on Mexicans—which became code for "immigrants," particularly non-white immigrants—began in his June 16, 2015, campaign announcement speech during which he stated that "[w]hen Mexico sends it people, they're not sending their best. [...] They're bringing drugs. They're bringing crime. They're rapists. And some, I assume, are good people" (Kopan, 2016). After the campaign, these comments became the foundation of Trump's foreign policy platform as president—to instill fear of the Other.

So, on November 9, 2016, I could report that I had sat with much of the world in shocked disbelief and sadness the previous night as I had watched the election results come in, declaring Donald Trump as our country's 45th President. It was a sleepless night as I lay awake thinking of the possibility of harmful campaign promises kept. That morning of November 9 was chilly and crisp, and as I walked into Washington River High School, a former teacher turned teacher educator and researcher, I noticed the stillness of the air—as if the world were holding its breath.

There, Mrs. Carina Durham, a high school teacher to English Language Learners (ELLs) in Washington River, an exurban community in Nebraska in which a large number of Latinx[1] immigrants live and work, faced her students on the morning following the election with a brief acknowledgement of the election results.[2] Her normally boisterous and animated disposition was muted on this day. Mrs. Gabriela Sánchez, the Spanish-English bilingual paraeducator who worked alongside Mrs. Durham, served as a translator and interpreter in the classroom.

---

[1] Following DeGuzmán (2017), I use the inclusive gender-neutral and non-binary "Latinx," except in reference to census data that uses "Hispanic or Latino."

[2] English Language Learner (ELL) is used to refer to students who are in the process of learning English (Wright, 2010), and, while deficit-based terminology (defining a category based on what a student does not know), it was the language used by Washington River High School and Mrs. Durham and I use it here to reflect that. This term arose as a counter to the label of Limited English Proficient (LEP), which is even more deficit-based. According to the 1974 *Lau v. Nichols* Supreme Court ruling (1974), all students have a right to instruction in a language they understand; that is, *equal* instruction (i.e., instruction in English for all students) does not equate to equal educational opportunity. Title III of the No Child Left Behind Act (NCLB) of 2001 replaced bilingual education with Language Instruction for Limited English Proficient and Immigrant Students (Wright, 2010), and in doing so, English was privileged above other languages for the purposes of education.

Preface • xi

She was usually more reserved than Mrs. Durham, but on this day her demeanor seemed a mixture of anger and numbness. Having just finished a brief curriculum unit on elections in the United States in their United States history class—and even holding their own mock election the day before—they were tasked on that Wednesday with helping their students make sense of what might be next.

On that day following Trump's election, both educators faced a classroom full of newcomer immigrant and migrant students who had just a couple of days earlier nervously joked about the prospects of being deported to help build Trump's proposed wall.[3] Their students were quiet, consoling friends with a touch on the arm or a brief hug before sitting in their desks. These students, many of whom were undocumented[4] or in the process of seeking asylee status[5] and others who came from 'mixed status' households where parents or siblings lacked documentation and were vulnerable, were the very portrait of the immigrants Trump had targeted and vilified during his campaign. Their slumped shoulders and downcast eyes conveyed their understanding of the implications of this election for their lives.

The members of Mrs. Durham's history class entered a dark classroom and could see that their teacher had been crying. Mrs. Sánchez sat solemnly behind her desk. When the students were seated, Mrs. Durham took a deep and shaky breath. I imagined it must have felt like the first words she would speak to these students bore the weight of the world—and their futures. "I know today is going to be really hard for some of you," she began slowly. "I want you to remember that based on the government we have, no one person has all the power." Her voice broke as she held tears at bay. She took a deep breath and continued, "If anything happens to you..." she trailed off, paused, and then continued, "...this room will always be a safe place." Many students smiled. They were all silent as they listened to Mrs. Sánchez translate into Spanish what Mrs. Durham had said. Mrs. Durham went on, "I don't have a very large basement ...but I do have a basement. You can come live with me." There were many giggles in the room after students heard Mrs. Sánchez's translation. "I love you guys very much," she finished. Alejandro's quiet "Thank you, Mrs. Durham" sounded loud in the hushed room.

---

[3] Trump, during his 2015 announcement of his candidacy for president promised, "I would build a great wall [on our southern border]—and nobody builds walls better than me, believe me—and I'll build them very inexpensively. I will build a great, great wall on our southern border. And I will have Mexico pay for that wall" (Kopan, 2016).

[4] "Undocumented" refers to a person residing in the United States "without legal permission" (Abrego & Gonzales, 2010, p. 145).

[5] "Asylee status" is granted to a person who, after arriving in the U.S., seeks protection from persecution based on race, religion, national origin, gender, political opinion, or on being a part of a particular social group. The F4 category of family-based sponsorships for green cards is a recent development for those fleeing El Salvador, Honduras, and Guatemala (Justice for Our Neighbors, personal communication, October 6, 2017).

xii • LEARNING TO HIDE

Less than three months later, the first executive actions of the Trump presidency validated the fears and tears in Mrs. Durham's classroom that day. The executive order to authorize the construction of the border wall Trump had promised from his campaign podium between the United States and Mexico—the border all these students had crossed—was issued just days after Trump's inauguration (Executive Order No. 13767, 2017). Days later, Trump's next order banning the entry of refugees from seven majority-Muslim countries sent another clear message. The Trump administration meant to instill fear of—and in—immigrants, especially those from war-torn and violence-ridden regions (Executive Order No. 13769, 2017). The chaos that ensued at airports and in protest marches across the country (and the world) were different manifestations of the feelings these students experienced quietly on November 9.

* * *

Democracy is a fragile endeavor, dependent as it is on participation and a commitment to the capital 'p' Public. It was especially so in a highly polarized context of the United States in 2016 and 2017, and even more so as I finished this manuscript in 2023. Neoliberal conceptions of citizens as consumers cultivates competition among citizens and affirms the ideological notion of rugged individualism, undergirding and thwarting even progressive efforts in education (Sharma et al., 2023). Civic engagement through community organizations has declined (Levine, 2007; Putnam, 2000), and in 2016, voters seemed apathetic about their efficacy through the ballot box (trends that reversed moderately in the 2018 mid-terms and 2020 presidential election). Back in 2016 and still as I wrote these words in 2023, members of Congress and the public in general were so politically "polarized"—voting and collaborating strictly along party lines and even arguing within those divides—as to prevent any sort of democratic deliberation at all, and an ethos of winning and losing prevails (Fiorina & Abrams, 2008; Hess & McAvoy, 2015).[6]

In the midwestern U.S. community of Washington River, demographic change has forced longstanding residents to encounter and interact with people who are socially, culturally, and linguistically different from one another. This often has not gone well. Immigrants—especially immigrants in Brown bodies—have been criminalized in both *de facto* and *de jure* ways (Santa Ana, 2002). Polarization paralyzes the cultivation of the public spaces where deliberation over public issues ought to happen. Instead, deliberation is thwarted by the noise and financial resources of the powerful and wealthy groups who pose almost insurmountable

---

[6] For example, two years into the presidency of Joe Biden, conservative justices dominate the U.S. Supreme Court, justices who have decided pivotal cases that returned to states the power to limit and/or ban reproductive healthcare, allowed for businesses to deny services to customers on the basis of religious beliefs, and declared affirmative action unconstitutional (Liptak, July 1, 2023).

Preface • **xiii**

political obstacles to grassroots democratic action.[7] The struggles of historically marginalized groups to claim rights—especially because Trump's presidency and enduring influence emboldened previously suppressed nationalist, nativist, sexist, and racist rhetoric—has resulted in a deeper divide in the social landscape.

Donald Trump's 2016 election to the presidency was a symptom of the fissures in the sociopolitical context of the United States. As I write these words only a couple of years after Trump has left office after an acrimonious lame duck period punctuated by the Big Lie about (nonexistent) electoral fraud and the related subsequent siege of the Capitol on January 6, 2021, it is clear that his administration's policies and rhetoric profoundly deepened the divides in U.S. society. In fact, I wrote a large part of this manuscript from my home due to his administration's inept response to a quickly spreading coronavirus pandemic in 2020. The economic crisis resulting from the pandemic shutdown has crippled the country and exposed the dramatic wealth, education, and workforce disparities between people in different racial groups (Wilson, 2020).

Protests erupted in the summer of 2020 following the murder of George Floyd, a Black man, by a white police officer as he knelt on Floyd's neck for nine minutes and twenty-nine seconds[8]—even as Floyd cried out that he couldn't breathe. People have taken to the streets to protest police brutality against and the murder of Black people by police. People have taken to social media to argue about whether All Lives Matter or if, in this moment, we could agree that all lives cannot matter *unless* Black Lives Matter. We are arguing about the politics of seeing color and raising societal consciousness about the implications of seeing color. In this historical moment, citizenship—the daily practice of living alongside others—is of special import. What kind of citizen does this country need to reclaim and sustain a democratic nation?

Democracy is not a static enterprise. Democracy—characterized by John Dewey (1916) as a "mode of associated living"—requires a citizenry who attend to all people's right to a "good life." We need citizens who can engage in productive dialogue and deliberation to understand one another and overcome political polarization. We need citizens who acknowledge each other's equal humanity, and who understand that their own freedom is interconnected with and dependent upon others' freedom. We need citizens who understand that we must seek out,

---

[7] The Supreme Court ruling in the *Citizens United v. Federal Election Commission* case in 2010 granted wealthy groups the legal right to wield financial resources for political goals. This ruling that "spending is speech" effactually granted corporations the same rights as people, allowing corporations to spend unlimited amounts of money to persuade voters (i.e., through campaign ads or propaganda) as long as they do not give money directly to candidates (Dunbar, 2012). The financial resources at the disposal of a large corporation clearly dwarf those of individuals or other less-wealthy groups, thereby privileging corporate interests (e.g., regulations and political agreements involving in their industries) over those of individuals.

[8] Earlier accounts of this event reported that the officer had knelt on Floyd's neck for eight minutes and 46 seconds, a time estimate frequently repeated and even made popular as a design for COVID masks (Bogel-Burroughs, 2021).

not shield ourselves from, different perspectives to attain equality for all citizens. We need citizens who hear each other and see each other as humans deserving of equal rights and being accountable to one another. We need citizens who can think critically about the social constructions that thwart equality. We need a conceptualization of an inclusive "we." That includes an understanding of citizenship that is not narrowly legalistic, but more expansive and foundational to mean membership in and responsiveness to a community.

Understood as a way of living together, democracy must be learned. Dewey (1916) argued that education is a "midwife" of democracy, aiding in giving life to democracy with each successive generation. Thomas Jefferson in the 1700s and Benjamin Rush in the 1900s advocated for a system of public schools that would be seen as makers of citizens (Labaree, 2010). Schools in a democratic context, then, face a unique challenge in *consciously* producing citizens (and reproducing democracy) who can construct and practice democracy in a justice-oriented way (Allen, 2004; Gutmann, 1987).[9] Because schools are "the first sustained *public* experience for children" (Parker, 2003, p. xviii), it follows that they are sites for democratic education and political engagement.

However, social actors in schools perform "cultural scripts" (Gutiérrez et al., 1995) and perpetuate majoritarian stories (Love, 2004)[10] that undergird *evasion pedagogies* which "evade solving the fundamental problem of inequity in our schools and society through the project of teaching and learning" (Viesca & Gray, 2021, p. 214). Evasion pedagogies serve to sustain white supremacy and other forms of oppression within the institution of schooling by (1) emphasizing image over substance (i.e., attending to how something appears over what actually is), (2) the power of boundaries and limited relationships (i.e., maintaining hierarchies and distinct roles of teachers and students), and (3) the perpetuation of majoritarian stories and cultural scripts (i.e., performances of "best practices").

This book is a story of how newcomer students—young immigrants and migrants who have newly arrived in the United States—in an English Language Learner (ELL) social studies classroom at Washington River High School constructed citizen identities within this context of political polarization, nativism, racism, and nationalism. This story documents events from 2016, but many of the experiences detailed within endure into 2023. While this is not a fully optimistic account, it offers useful lessons for disrupting evasion pedagogies toward an aim of teaching and learning that fosters belonging for all students.

---

[9] My use of the word "citizen" refers to all people who are guaranteed equal protection of rights under the 14th Amendment of the Constitution of the United States; that is, all people living in the U.S. *regardless of legal status* (Chomsky, 2007; Levinson, 2012).

[10] B. J. Love (2004) defines majoritarian stories as "the description of events as told by members of dominant/majority groups, accompanied by values and beliefs that justify the actions taken by dominants to insure their dominant position" (p. 228). As such, majoritarian stories are oppressive.

INTRODUCTION

MAYBERRY IN FLUX[1]

Just inside Washington River High School's doors from the rear parking lot, in the farthest reaches from the school's front entrance, there is a short corridor that leads to the hallway that houses the school's two English Learning classrooms. These classrooms offer both safe sanctuary for the school's growing population of Latinx students and a troublingly hidden space that allows most of the school and community to maintain the pretense of the generally prosperous, white, neighbor-helping-neighbor locale of their myopic nostalgia. This Mayberry-like imaginary excludes the divisive sociopolitical battles of the last fifteen years that have earned Washington River both local and national attention for a city ordinance that would fine landlords who rented to undocumented residents, a *de jure* policy that led to *de facto* racial profiling. The English Learning classrooms are thus sites for the work of learning English and other academic subjects alongside the more abstract but no less important work of constructing citizen identities. In these spaces, adolescent Latinx newcomers negotiate and assert complicated claims about how

[1] Mayberry references the idyllic and fictitious small-town featured in the 1960 sitcom *The Andy Griffith Show*. While Mayberry was mainly modeled on Mount Airy, North Carolina (Griffith's hometown), an actual nearby town, Siler City, features in two of that show's episodes and as of 2018 Census bureau estimates it had become about 40% Latinx, making that the largest population group in the city (ahead of both non-Hispanic white people and African Americans). Readers can determine whether Washington River is more aptly compared to Mt. Airy or Siler City.

Learning to Hide: The English Learning Classroom as Sanctuary and Trap
pages xv–xxvi.
Copyright © 2024 by Information Age Publishing
www.infoagepub.com
All rights of reproduction in any form reserved.

they get to be *of* Washington River High School, the wider community, and, more holistically, the United States.

As longer established residents (practically all white) and almost exclusively Latinx newcomers have interacted with each other (or not) in Washington River, they have confronted people who are linguistically, culturally, racially, and socially different from themselves. The polarized and contentious sociopolitical context of the United States in the wake of Donald Trump's election to the United States presidency in 2016 provides the backdrop to this book. I center the experiences of newcomer students as they constructed citizen identities within the micro-context of their classroom and school and the macro-context of a changing and polarized United States.

While this is an account of the local context of Washington River, the issues raised—welcome, unwelcome, belonging, and claiming rights (Gitlin et al., 2003)—are not particular to Washington River. As part of the changing sociocultural landscape of the Midwestern United States in which historically distinct groups come together in common spaces, Washington River High School offers an example of the concurrently familiar and uncomfortable ways that *place* in the New Latinx Diaspora (NLD) gets negotiated—NLD referencing contexts in which Latinx newcomers had not traditionally settled in significant number prior to the final decades of the 20th Century (Hamann et al., 2002, 2015).

The meatpacking industry has drawn an increasing number of immigrants to Washington River from Mexico and Central America since the 1990s, making it a part of the NLD. Demographic change amidst the sociopolitical landscape of neoliberalism, declining civic engagement, and polarized partisan politics has forced interaction between longstanding white residents and almost exclusively Latinx newcomers. Historically marginalized groups have long sought to claim rights, including in Washington River, in response to the long sought (and still not passed) DREAM Act.[2] In response, especially upon Donald Trump's election to the U.S. presidency in 2016, there has been a xenophobic, white nationalist backlash resulting in deepening fissures in the social landscape of the country writ large and also in Washington River.

Within this divisive and complicated sociopolitical context, I wondered how newcomer high school students imagined themselves as citizens—small 'c' citizens who belong and could and would claim the full range of rights and responsibilities guaranteed by the Constitution of the United States (U.S. Const., amend. XIV, § 1). Washington River High School provided a context in which to explore questions about how NLD students construct citizen identities. How do high school newcomer students construct citizen identities in social studies, a program of study dedicated to providing opportunities for citizenship construction? Who

---

[2] The Development, Relief, and Education for Alien Minors (DREAM) Act was first introduced by Senators Dick Durbin and Orrin Hatch in 2001 and is considered a bipartisan effort to open pathways to conditional and legal residency for so-called Dreamers, people without legal status who immigrated to the United States before the age of 16 (American Immigration Council, 2021).

are key individuals who influence the construction of citizenship and how do they influence students? Finally, given the institutional nature of schooling, how do newcomers transform the school and how does the school transform them? By illuminating the experiences of Latinx newcomer students in this space, I have sought to explicitly interrogate the extent to which the conditions in which newcomers learn afford them opportunities to understand, claim, develop, and assert their human and civil rights and responsibilities as residents of the United States.[3]

While their classroom became a sanctuary—a sanctuary from the conspicuous mismatch between the newcomers and more established elements of the school and the community—it also became a kind of trap that kept students hidden from the larger school and community and deferred significant contestation of their structured subordination. Durable schooling structures and practices constructed dual realities for newcomer students (i.e., youth and adult, student and worker, belonging and exclusion) and revealed a stark mismatch between these dual realities and the life of the school. Additionally, the ways in which different multifaceted and multidimensional social actors manifested care indicated different aims for schooling and implied different conceptions of citizenship for newcomers. Finally, because of both the geographic and semiotic distance of their classroom from the 'heart' of the school, there were missed opportunities to connect the life and curriculum of the U.S. history class and broader school to these students' lives and to integrate them into the school and community in meaningful and justice-oriented ways. All these ideas illustrate the paradox of sanctuary and trap in this classroom—that newcomers needed sanctuary *from* a context in which their identities were not valued and sanctuary *for* a space in which they could be fully themselves. They reveal how this school relegated newcomers to the margins and thwarted equitable opportunities to construct citizen identities within the full realm of the school's public space and ideological public sphere.

The sanctuary and trap dynamic emerges because of the broader (i.e., largely white) fear and resistance to change in this NLD community and in the public high school that serves its residents. The ideology of whiteness—the privileging of English, the nativist rationale for excluding immigrants from full belonging, and the deficit-based justification for segregated schooling arrangements (i.e., ELL program) (Matias, 2016)—undergirded the life and work inside Washington River High School and in the community of Washington River. Social actors in the school and community performed carefully curated cultural and social "scripts" (Gutiérrez et al., 1995) grounded in whiteness. Whiteness undergirded even the racist conservative yearning for the Mayberry-esque community many thought they remembered from before Brown-bodied immigrants began arriving in significant numbers.

---

[3] Readers can find a more detailed methodology of this study in my dissertation (Hagen Gray, 2017), accessible here: https://digitalcommons.unl.edu/dissertations/AAI10682492/

xviii • LEARNING TO HIDE

THE CONTEXT OF IMMIGRATION
AND THE NEW LATINX DIASPORA

Although new arrivals from Mexico tapered nationally and locally in the second decade of the 21st Century (Boehm, 2016), large numbers of immigrants from the Northern Triangle countries of Central America—i.e., Guatemala, El Salvador, and Honduras—continued to arrive, joining second-generation Mexican immigrants (Pew Research Center, 2014a). The reasons undergirding immigration from the Northern Triangle are complex and largely related to the decades of poverty and violence in the home countries, much of which was brought on by United States destabilizing involvement in these countries (Pew Research Center, 2014b).[4] As a dynamic that again flared at the beginning of the Biden administration, in the 2010s the number of unaccompanied and/or undocumented minors entering the United States seeking employment or reunification with family members has grown steadily (Catalano, 2017). Many of them speak Indigenous languages instead of or in addition to Spanish and a significant majority have had only four to five years of formal schooling in their home countries (Catholic Relief Services, 2010).

New Latinx Diaspora (NLD)

The New Latinx Diaspora (NLD) is used to describe new contexts in which Latinx immigrants and migrants settle—both in the short and long term (Hamann & Harklau, 2015). The term also denotes the "improvised interethnic interaction" that occurs in these contexts when Latinx newcomers enter spaces in the school and community they have not previously occupied, as well as the negotiation of new norms for non-Latinx residents (Hamann et al., 2002, p. 1). In addition, it signifies the makeshift and impromptu nature of the responses that often become institutionalized. More recently, Hamann and Harklau (2021) have critically noted that a phenomenon that is now 20+ years old too often remains improvisational, suggesting neglect or low prioritization rather than surprise.

The Midwestern United States in general and Nebraska in particular are home to industries that attract immigrants (i.e., agriculture, construction, manufacturing, and food processing), especially in rural areas, and Washington River, a midwestern meatpacking center, has become a NLD context in the past thirty years (Hamann & Harklau, 2015). The challenges to public services (e.g., schools and health care facilities) in these areas—lacking financial resources and experience in working with immigrant families—have prompted mostly improvised responses to the arrival of immigrants and migrants (Bruening, 2015; Bigelow, 2010; Hamann & Harklau, 2015; Harklau & Colomer, 2015; Reeves, 2004). This

---

[4] For example, Honduras' murder rate, attributed to violence stemming from gangs and drug trafficking, was almost 90 homicides per 100,000 residents in 2012, and has hovered near that number since then. This was the highest rate in the world at the time of this study (Pew Research Center, 2014b; U.S. Department of State, 2017).

is especially true in schools where the language of instruction is only English[5] and there are few Teachers of English to Speakers of Other Languages (TESOL), interpreters, and translators, much less bilingual teachers, and where the graduation rates of "Hispanic"[6] students are substantially lower than the number of Hispanic students enrolled in high school (Bruening, 2015; Hamann, 2002; Hamann & Harklau, 2015; Harklau & Colomer, 2015; Reeves, 2004).

I made my home in Washington River at the time of this study and before, having arrived in 2007. As a Spanish-English bilingual, white, female high school Spanish teacher at Washington River High School, I lived the "improvised inter-ethnic interaction" (Hamann et al., 2002) myself. Indeed, one of my first tasks was to try to enact a more equitable language-learning experience for my already-fluent Spanish-speaking students seeking to earn world language credits for graduation. Securing approval for this course from the school district's curriculum committee involved thorough planning in anticipation of a negative response from community members concerned that teaching resources were to be allocated to a specific group of students (and presumably to non-English-dominant students). We proposed several iterations of just the title of the class before the one that was finally selected and proposed to the school board so that it would be less obvious to whom the class would be aimed and offered (i.e., Spanish for Proficient Speakers).[7] The school board unanimously accepted our proposal and this achievement was the front page headline in the community's local newspaper the following day. Although I no longer work at Washington River High School, I have remained in close contact with the community, and this extended life experience of being *among* and *with* the people of this particular cultural site has provided unique opportunities to understand the cultural and social "scripts" that undergird life in Washington River (Gutiérrez et al., 1995).

"Save Our City": The Local Context of Washington River

Washington River, an industrial community of just over 26,000 residents and the local county seat, is located in the exurbs of a large Midwestern metropolitan city and has experienced significant demographic change since the 1990s with the arrival of increased numbers of immigrants, mainly of Mexican and other Latinx

---

[5] In recent years and after my field study was completed, the Washington River school district implemented a Spanish-English dual language program at one elementary school, starting with one kindergarten class and adding a grade level as the inaugural class progressed through elementary school.

[6] "Hispanic" is a contested term with racializing connotations (Oboler, 2006; Chomsky, 2007), but I use it here to reflect the demographic categories used by the United States Census Bureau (2010), Pew Research Center (2015), and the school's data. All ethnic and/or racial terminology is subject to debate.

[7] Previous iterations of the class name that were decided against for various reasons included Spanish for Heritage Speakers, Spanish for Native Speakers, and Spanish for Heritage Learners. In all cases, the curriculum committee of the district weighed the aptness of the course description against potential words (i.e., heritage, native) that might flag the attention of conservative community watchdogs.

origins. The city's meatpacking plants have played a significant role in attracting immigrants to the community. The town of Riverview, located just to the south, has been absorbed physically into the community of Washington River, separated only by the still-active railroad tracks over which a viaduct serves as the primary linkage between the two communities. That viaduct carries a state highway over the tracks and then through the middle of the community, with the viaduct rising as one of the only "hills" in the otherwise nearly flat landscape. Washington River's proximity to highway and rail networks make it attractive to meatpacking corporations for distribution purposes.

Washington River's economy is based mainly in the areas of agribusiness, food processing, fabricated metal processing, and electronics manufacturing. The community's public school system and two nearby meatpacking plants employ a significant number of residents; a disproportionate number of recent immigrants and migrants work in the meatpacking plants and school system employees are mainly white, excepting bilingual paraprofessionals like Mrs. Sánchez and a few others. Washington River is also close enough to two metropolitan areas that a large number of residents commute to work in those areas. The median household income of Washington River's residents was around $43,000 between 2006 and 2010, which was slightly lower than the Nebraska state average (U.S. Census Bureau, 2010). Fourteen percent of all persons fell below the poverty level for that same time frame, which was just over two percent higher than the state's total. A large majority of the town's residents lived in owner-occupied housing units.

A controversial anti-immigration ordinance[8] in Washington River less than a decade before the 2016 national election revealed the conservative (and white supremacist) impulse to keep out or at least subordinate anyone who threatened the status quo. The ordinance was an effort by a small but shrill and powerful group to ban the "harboring, hiring, and renting to illegal aliens." This effort was polarizing and carried undertones of racist motivations, evidenced by one early piece of propaganda I received in the mail citing informally gathered statistics about the impact of "illegal immigrants" in the community (e.g., noting that a disproportionate number of "Hispanic-looking" clients utilized the emergency room at the city's only hospital, where all patients must be treated, even if they cannot pay for services). The mailing even equated the enforcement of laws against "illegal" immigration with the enforcement of traffic laws and ended by urging residents like me to "save our city."

That ordinance passed by special election in the summer of 2010 but after legal challenges by the American Civil Liberties Union (ACLU) and the Mexican American Legal Defense and Educational Fund (MALDEF), the court ruled out only the provision banning renting to "illegal aliens," and therefore, the ordinance prohibiting the "harboring and hiring of illegal aliens" in Washington River was enacted. The debate surrounding this issue both in the lead-up to and in the re-

---

[8] I withhold citations for the ordinance to mask the name of the community of Washington River.

Mayberry in Flux • xxi

sponse to the vote was polarizing and revealed deep divisions in the community, as people on both sides of the issue defended their stances and garnered national attention.

Proponents of the ordinance claimed that "illegal aliens" ought to be held accountable for breaking federal immigration laws, noting the federal government's failure to enforce these laws. While they maintained that this was not a racially motivated act, opponents, organizing under the banner 'one Washington River, one community,' disagreed. They pointed out the relatively small number of immigrants living within the city limits who were undocumented and expressed concern about what they perceived to be a xenophobic message the ordinance was sending to all persons of Hispanic or Latinx origin, regardless of immigration status.

Indeed, this local ordinance prompted considerable attention to the need for immigration reform and to the ideological underpinnings of our current immigration system. Additionally, it illuminated how civilians both for and against the ordinance positioned themselves as protectors of their communities, although it was only the pro-ordinance side that framed immigrants as threatening.

A PUBLIC GATHERING PLACE:
WASHINGTON RIVER HIGH SCHOOL

Required by precedent and law to serve all portions of this polarized community, Washington River Public Schools served just under 5,000 students in thirteen schools at the time of my study, including seven Kindergarten-through-fourth-grade elementary schools, two middle schools (one for fifth- and sixth-grades and one for seventh- and eighth grades), and one comprehensive high school. There were also a small alternative high school and a preschool center. Schools, as public spaces that bring together diverse young citizens, have the opportunity to develop a shared community for all students. Washington River High School (WRHS) was a four-year high school with an enrollment of 1,381 students in grades 9–12 for 2014–2015 (the year before I entered WRHS for my study), with 85 teaching faculty members, one principal, two assistant principals, and four guidance counselors.

The WRHS guidance counselors in 2016 were all monolingual English speakers. Despite the growing numbers of Spanish-speaking families and students, a Spanish-English bilingual counselor had been passed over in a recent hiring process for a monolingual English speaker who was previously a science teacher at the school. A teacher who took on the role of football coach as well then filled the vacancy in the science department. Aside from the five Spanish teachers in the school, there were no other teachers who spoke Spanish fluently.[9] There were two

---

[9] There was, however, a Spanish-English bilingual mathematics teacher who had recently retired. In her tenure at WRHS, she regularly taught her math courses bilingually with tremendous success. Her retirement left a gaping absence in opportunities for Spanish-dominant students in math courses.

xxii • LEARNING TO HIDE

bilingual paraeducators who worked with teachers of English Language Learners (ELLs) and in the in-school student assistance center—the Panthers Achievement Center, or "PAC room." The school advertised for a third bilingual paraeducator position just after I concluded my research at the school.

The school building itself was a sprawling two-level structure with hallways branching off from a central lobby area around the main office. Although I had been a Spanish teacher at this school for four years, I had been gone for five years at the beginning of the study, and I made the following observations as I entered the school for the first time since leaving.

A crisp fall Wednesday. The sun—low in the sky—shines brightly over the corner of the brick building and peeks through the massive stone pillars flanking the entrance to the school. Cars jerk and stop in the morning traffic on the crowded street in front of the school, coffee mug-gripping parents hunched behind the wheel. Groggy-eyed students with still-damp hair jump out of cars in the middle of the street—the congestion does not allow space to pull off the street to drop off students. Most students carry nothing; some carry a small sack backpack on their shoulders.

A small group of students stands in the church parking lot opposite the school front, borrowing lighters and bumming cigarettes from each other; each of them wears a dark-colored hoodie, hood up and sleeves pulled down low over their non-cigarette-holding hand. They glance my way but take little notice of me. A police car swings into the parking lot entrance beside them and the students scatter, but slowly. They pick up the books they had stacked on the ground and mosey away down the sidewalk. Still-burning cigarettes lay littering the grass next to the parking lot, abandoned when the police car shows up.

This group is a reiteration of the same group every year. The church parking lot stands directly across from the school, but it is not school property; as such, students cannot be held to school rules (i.e., an eighteen-year-old can legally smoke in public but not in school). When I was teaching at the school, there was very little concern about this. The church members express their concern perennially about the trash and cigarette butts these students leave behind on their property—but not necessarily about the tobacco use in young adults.

As I approach the building entrance, I notice small groups of students huddled together, some eating granola bars, and others wrap two hands around their thermal mugs and pull the mugs close to their faces. One student bumps shoulders with the person next to him while another runs with arms outstretched toward an approaching girl. "Miranda! I missed you!" she exclaims and wraps Miranda in a hug.

I approach the front door at the same time as a student; we glance at each other, and I reach for the door. As I open the glass door (hoping it was the correct unlocked door), the student slips silently past me. The wide foyer of the school entrance is filled with the bright morning sunshine streaming through two-story windows and reflecting off the white floor tiles.

I sign in as a visitor to the building, writing my name, the date, and the time I enter. The woman behind the split window writes my name on a "VISITOR" nametag sticker. She peels it off *(laboriously)* and hands it through the window to me. I stick it to the upper left shoulder of my sweater and with that, I turn in the direction of the classroom.

I proceeded through the lobby space lined with wood-paneled walls and benches and then through the hall aptly nicknamed the "Fishbowl." The floor-to-ceiling windows on either side of the "Fishbowl" hallway allowed the sunlight to stream across the entire width of the area, and the five short rows of beige-painted lockers that stood in the middle of the hallway and perpendicular to the windows cast long shadows across the beige tiles. Midway through this hallway were black tiles inset in a pattern spelling out the initials of the school.

The school was generally—perhaps superficially—welcoming, the airy and bright entrance giving way to dimmer, more artificially lit, brick-lined corridors farther from the main entrance. Some staff members stood smiling and greeting students as they held their cups of coffee, while others rushed between their classrooms and the main office area, making last-minute preparations for the day. This first morning proved to be a typical day at the school, and I often waved to the same teachers in the main lobby upon my arrival on subsequent days.

SOCIAL STUDIES AS A SITE FOR
DEMOCRATIC CITIZENSHIP EDUCATION

Democratic citizenship education is an explicit aim of the curricular program of social studies (Rubin, 2012). Thus, social studies classes provided a fruitful context in which to explore questions about how students learn democracy and construct citizen identities. The field of social studies, with the aim of citizen development, is an important course of study for all young people, but perhaps even more so for newcomer students (Abu El-Haj, 2007). Newcomers in the fraught sociopolitical context of 2016–17 and beyond need to claim "identity, space, and rights" by navigating the social, economic, and political systems of this country to ensure that they have a role in negotiating the rules by which we all live (Flores & Benmayor, 1997; Ladson-Billings, 2004; Oboler, 2006). Likewise, longstanding residents need to be able and willing to interrogate and sacrifice their own privilege accorded by their identities, space, and rights in a culture that privileges whiteness if we are to disrupt the ideological underpinnings that thwart more just and equitable lives for all citizens. (Describing this as a needed condition does not mean that it was a common one.)

Immigrant students, given their transnational experiences, often navigate a disconnect between citizenship and belonging (Abu El-Haj, 2009; Siham Fernández, 2021). However, schools in NLD receiving communities have the potential to be sites for the development of citizen identities oriented toward critical practices. Thea Abu El-Haj (2009) asserts that "[p]articipation and critical engagement,

xxiv • LEARNING TO HIDE

rather than a sense of national identification, may, in the end, prove a stronger base for developing engaged and active young citizens working for a more just and peaceful future for nations across the globe" (p. 81). Ten years after she wrote those words, the Trump administration had so hyped nationalist rhetoric that Abu El-Haj's wisdom may have become of even greater relevance and import as I was writing up my study than when she initially articulated it.

Newcomers at Washington River High School took social studies in a "sheltered" format (Short, 2002), essentially segregated from the rest of the student body. This sheltered approach had the stated purpose of supporting ELLs in content learning with extra language supports, although Valdés's (2001) critique that newcomers' language learning was inhibited when they were kept away from fluent speakers is important to acknowledge. Between September and December of 2016, I attended the class three days each week, observing, interviewing, and being helpful where I could be. My formal intent was to explore how newcomers in a sheltered ELL American history class at WRHS constructed citizen identities in that space. That is a main topic here too, although the benefit of time for a broader perspective and the serendipity of what else one discovers when engaged in ethnographic inquiry mean this text is relevant beyond just its illumination of newcomers' learning. Positioned within the extant sociopolitical context (i.e., nativist and nationalist anti-immigration policies, polarization, and marginalization and of languages other than English [Abedi, 2004; Santa Ana, 2002] and the racialization of speakers of languages other than English [Rosa, 2019]), Washington River High School afforded me a unique context in which to understand the social construction of citizenship as a lived experience for young people in school and to juxtapose that with the expectations held for other students and dominant community discourses about what kind of place Washington River was to be.

My preconceived notions of citizenship were unrecognizable in that space, and my attention shifted to the more nuanced relational, emotional, and cultural expressions of citizenship in the everyday. Raising up the experiences of newcomers and amplifying the voices of historically marginalized and minoritized people—especially in a site where pockets of the community project vitriolic and xenophobic responses to them—centers the lived experiences of newcomers. But those experiences come in a community context where welcome, inclusion, and membership are all contested. I attempt to capture the understandings of the students and educators who were gracious enough to permit me to be part of their lives, but I also bring the perspectives of an adult, former teacher, local resident, and (sometimes uncomfortable) member of the dominant culture that allow me to juxtapose what the newcomers see and seek with how they are seen and placed.

OUTLINE OF THE BOOK

This book aims to draw on the experiences of the newcomers in this study and my own as I engaged with the community to provide wisdom and insight into how we might co-construct a more equitable and just democratic society. In Chapter

One, I provide an overview of policies that influence the school lives of newcomers, and I describe the English Language Learning (ELL) program at Washington River High School, including the curriculum and structure of the specific sheltered-ELL U.S. history class in which I observed. Given the ideological nature of curriculum (Apple, 2014) and the political work of schools (Nieto & Bode, 2012), I also examine what these structures and curriculum help us understand about the values of the school and community.

In Chapter Two, I introduce the students, the teacher, and the paraeducator who bring the space to life, and I explore the identities that they brought to school and how those identities influenced the life of the classroom. In Chapter Three, I describe the classroom culture and discuss the physical, social-emotional, and cognitive dimensions of sanctuary as they were constructed and manifested in the classroom.

Chapters Four through Six describe various realities of the classroom and school and explore how these realities influence the construction of citizen identities in the space. In Chapter Four, I explore how both the wider context of the school and community and the classroom communities were a "mismatch" that revealed the dualities of newcomers' lived experiences (Deschenes et al., 2001). The stagnant and monolithic nature of the curriculum, and the way the curriculum was mediated erased the biographies of the students, creating the 'everyday ruptures' that Hamann and Zúñiga (2011) have described transnational students in Mexico similarly negotiating. These multidimensional mismatches conveyed a dominant culture's view that the school was not theirs and that their one-directional assimilation was the goal. Chapter Five offers perspectives of how different people expressed care in different ways, which constructed sanctuary in the classroom, but which also implied differing conceptions of citizenship and aims for schooling. Chapter Six describes the multiple missed opportunities in curriculum and practice for a more deliberate cultivation of democratic citizenship to foster belonging in the wider school and community.

In Chapter Seven, I critique the classroom as sanctuary to argue that the safety of the space was concurrently a trap. I discuss how mismatch, varying notions of care, and missed opportunities contributed to creating and sustaining the trap, and I interrogate the implications for the construction of citizen identities in this space in which "learning to hide" was a central practice. Further, I critique how the school's resistance to change holds fast the trap and explore what the various social actors learn when this trap persists. I resituate this work of constructing citizenship in a Brown body during a time of emboldened racism and discrimination amplified by the rhetoric and policies of then-President Trump and I interrogate the conditions in this school and classroom in which students learn to hide and to remain on the margins of the public realm. In doing so, I describe the "evasion pedagogies" (Viesca & Gray, 2021) performed and perpetuated in this school that thwarted education as a humanizing and liberatory practice (Freire, 1970).

xxvi • LEARNING TO HIDE

I conclude in Chapter Eight with major lessons learned from the experiences of the people in this ELL social studies classroom and offer questions to guide reflection about what *better* might look like. I consider implications for curriculum and instruction, school culture, community resources, and corporate responsibility toward the aim of disrupting the evasion pedagogies at play in the school. I take up the call on the newcomers' t-shirts to "hear us, see us" and examine the conditions that necessitate sanctuary and perpetuate the trap and ask, what might it mean to hear and see newcomer students? What might it look like to deliberately foster democratic citizenship practices that cultivate belonging?

CHAPTER 1

THE POLITICAL WORK OF THE ELL[1] PROGRAM AT WRHS

The policies and practices of a school reveal the values undergirding their work (Apple, 2014; Jackson, 1968). In Washington River High School (WRHS), the school policies regarding graduation requirements were grounded in the belief that English proficiency preceded content learning. The age-out limitation of public schooling (wherein students with a high school degree may stay enrolled in high school until age 21) posed a challenge to newcomers to beat the clock to earn graduation credits before they aged out of the school system. Thus, the goal of accumulating credits quickly superseded the project of learning to be critical thinkers and agents in constructing a more equitable society. The curriculum, too, manifested the school's evasion of responsibility to engage in the project of democracy in which all people are regarded as citizens.

THE ELL PROGRAM AT WRHS

Newcomer immigrant and migrant students at WRHS were tested for English proficiency when they enrolled at the school because English was the sole lan-

---

[1] WRHS used the term English Language Learning/Learner (ELL) to describe multilingual students who were placed in classes to learn English. I use this term and the shortened "English Learning/Learner" (EL) to reflect the school's language.

Learning to Hide: The English Learning Classroom as Sanctuary and Trap
pages 1–12.
Copyright © 2024 by Information Age Publishing
www.infoagepub.com
All rights of reproduction in any form reserved.

1

2 • LEARNING TO HIDE

guage of instruction in all courses, except in the world language (i.e., Spanish and German) and Spanish for Proficient Speakers classes in which instructors used a blend of English and the target language. Identified English Language Learners (ELLs) (or English Learners [ELs]) comprised 4.34% of the student population in the 2014–15 school year at WRHS, according to the state Department of Education. In 2015 alone, there was an increase in the number of immigrant students who came to Washington River as unaccompanied minors seeking asylum, according to Mrs. Durham. Mrs. Sánchez told me after I concluded my observations in 2016 that later that academic year they welcomed almost forty new students into the program over a span of two months. When new students who did not speak English proficiently registered at the school they were tested in English proficiency and placed into one of four levels in the program: newcomer, beginner, intermediate, and advanced. The newcomer and beginner levels had ELL classes every day at the appropriate levels, and sheltered classes in mathematics, science, social studies, and English Language Arts (ELA)—all in one of the two full-time ELL classrooms. Intermediate students had one class a day in ELL during which they received assistance on core course materials (i.e., English, history, mathematics, and science).[2]

There were 105 students who qualified for an ELL class—levels 1 (newcomer) and 2 (beginner)—during the semester of my fieldwork. An additional 34 students were on a "tracking/monitor" status, which meant that Mrs. Durham needed to keep track of their progress and to intervene when necessary, even though they were no longer supported with ELL classes. There were, thus, a total of 139 students in the program at the high school, with two full-time ELL teachers (teaching three 88-minute classes per day) and two part-time ELL teachers (teaching one class per day). Considering the substantial amount of paperwork required to maintain for each student in the program, this was a sizeable load. By comparison, the middle school in the district employed just one full-time ELL teacher at the middle school who had eight to twelve students at levels one and two.

The two full-time and two part-time teachers in the school's ELL program were considered a part of the World Language Department. Mrs. Sánchez, one of two of the school's full-time Spanish-English bilingual paraeducators, worked in the newcomer/beginner ELL classrooms. The school ran on a block schedule consisting of four 88-minute classes. ELL students took "sheltered" (Haneda, 2009; Short, 2002; Short et al., 2011) core classes—two from each of the full-time ELL teachers—thereby maintaining progress toward graduation while concurrently taking intensive English language classes. Sheltered classes are those in which

---

[2] To clarify, except when specifically referencing the ELL program, my use of 'newcomer' in this document is not meant to match Washington River Schools' use of the term to mark (low-level) English proficiency. Rather, in agreement with Hamann and Mitchell-McCollough (2019) that the term 'immigrant' steers conceptualization of who recent arrivals are and what they need, I use newcomer as a more neutral term (depicting a chronological fact) to juxtapose Washington River's Latinx recent arrivals from the longer-established white population.

"efforts are made to make grade-level academic content more accessible to ELLs through various instructional strategies" (Haneda, 2009, p. 339). The two full-time ELL teachers were certified in four content areas under the High Objective Uniform State Standard of Evaluation (HOUSSE) portfolio system, which granted certification to ELL teachers who had earned the requisite number of college credits for each content area. This special certification—established by No Child Left Behind (2002) legislation—permits students to earn content-area credits for their work in their ELL classes. To this end, the school had adopted middle school-level *Access* textbooks in math, science, ELA, and American history that aligned with high school curriculum standards.

Mrs. Durham, in whose classroom I conducted this research, taught math and U.S. history to the newcomer/beginner students. The other full-time ELL teacher taught science and English language arts. While students were officially scheduled to have all four sheltered classes in one day, both teachers alternated the days on which they taught each of their content classes. For example, Mrs. Durham taught history in the 88-minute block one on Mondays and Wednesdays and taught math in the 88-minute block one on Tuesdays and Thursdays; block one on Fridays alternated between math and history. The other teacher alternated her schedule in the same way, but with science and ELA.

Three ELL classrooms (two full-time EL classrooms and one that split time between EL and special education) were located in one hallway of the school, and one was located on the opposite side of the building in the hallway with other English classes; the teacher who taught in the English classroom was assigned to teach general education English Language Arts (ELA) part-time and intermediate ELL part-time. Since the newcomer and beginner ELL students began their day in ELL classes, the hallway outside the full-time ELL classrooms was a "home base" to them. While some of them had lockers in this hallway, others shared those lockers—a single locker sometimes holding up to five students' materials. Each morning ELL students crowded the hallway waiting for the arrival of their teachers, and while some non-ELL students had assigned lockers in this hallway, it was seldom that non-ELL students passed through or stopped for more than a few seconds there.

The Structure of the Day

The majority of the ELL students normally arrived at school before 7:30 a.m.—well ahead of the 7:50 a.m. start of classes—and lined the hallway outside Mrs. Durham's classroom. I observed that this hallway was the ELL students' "neighborhood" because very few non-ELL students even walked through it, opting instead to travel through another parallel hallway to get from one side of the school to the other. Spanish words and phrases characterized the quiet din of the morning wait for classes to begin, and spoken English was a relatively rare and marked difference.

4 • LEARNING TO HIDE

Mrs. Durham's and the other full-time ELL teacher, Mrs. Burton's, classrooms faced each other from opposite sides of this hallway. The four-block schedule meant that general education students completed an academic year's worth of credits in one semester, but the alternating schedule of the sheltered ELL content classes meant that it took newcomer ELL students a full year to complete the course credits for each of four classes: science, math, ELA, and history.

Approximately half of the newcomer students (38 students total at the start of my fieldwork although this number changed almost weekly) started their day in Mrs. Burton's classroom and the sheltered content alternated daily between science and ELA; the ELA class mirrored the general education 9th grade ELA class which aimed to improve grammar and vocabulary skills and to engage students in studying a novel. The other half of the newcomer students were placed in Mrs. Durham's alternating sheltered U.S. history and math classes for their first block. Students switched classrooms for second block, which meant that newcomer students juggled four classes within their first two blocks of the day throughout the week. Newcomer and beginner-level students had ELL class—with the explicit focus on English language development—during their third block, and they took varying general education (e.g., Physical Education) or elective classes (e.g., Spanish[3], Art) during fourth block. The students' lunch time depended on the classroom to which they were assigned during third block. Lunchtime (when students went to the school's cafeteria) and fourth block were the only times newcomer ELLs would typically venture outside of this hallway.

THE SOCIAL STUDIES CURRICULUM

School is a place where young people have the opportunity to co-construct the ways in which they will live together, and the primary aim of social studies as a curricular area within schools is to educate democratic citizens (Dewey, 1938; Gutmann, 1988; National Council for the Social Studies, 2013, 2016; Parker, 2003). Democracy must be nurtured and reproduced and reimagined to persist; indeed, it is democratic citizens who sustain a robust democracy, and schools that prepare democratic citizens. The context of school in which diverse students share a public space makes possible citizenship construction, with social studies a formal and intentional part of that effort.

Curriculum standards double as accountability measures for schools and define the content areas to be mastered (Posner, 2004). Standards set forth what it is that students ought to be able to know and do within a given curricular area. The social studies curriculum standards for Nebraska—constructed in 2012 and updated to a more progressive version in 2019 (after my fieldwork had been completed) by

---

[3] While there was a Spanish for heritage speakers class offered at WRHS, newcomers were typically placed instead into an introductory Spanish as a world language course (i.e., not an adapted course). The rationale was that it offered newcomers an opportunity to experience academic success.

teachers, administrators, parents, and other stakeholders—included four perspectives considered integral to the development of citizens:

- The *historical* perspective requires students to understand and apply knowledge of national, state, and world history;
- The *civic* perspective includes attention to American government and political systems;
- The *geographic* perspective explores "spatial patterns" in the world; and
- The *economic* perspective examines the way resources are produced and used, especially within the free market system.

Taken together, the standards listed within these four perspectives aim to prepare students to be informed and active citizens.

Social studies in the ELL classroom at WRHS focused on U.S. history and closely followed Duran et al.'s (2005) *Access American History* textbook. Mrs. Durham worked closely with the general education history teachers to align curriculum outcomes for the course. The content in this textbook was simplified and condensed, moving quickly through American history (beginning with just three lessons in the first unit on "The First Americans"), and Mrs. Durham's class typically moved through one unit in approximately three weeks. The text offered a broad overview of United States history and indicated a focus on "breadth over depth." For example, the first unit in the text included three lessons: "The First Americans," which described the settlement of the North American continent in just eight heavily-illustrated pages; "European Exploration," which explained how "the search for new trade routes" prompted Christopher Columbus's (and others') explorations of the Americas during the 1400s and 1500s; and "The Thirteen Colonies," which covered the establishment of the original thirteen colonies and the eventual expansion and colonization of what would become the United States. The first unit included a mere four paragraphs dedicated to explaining the so-called "slave trade."

The second unit of study explored in its first lesson the steps leading up to the American Revolution, including the writing of the Declaration of Independence (but made no reference to that declaration's assertion of Britain's support of the "the merciless Indian Savages" as a motive for independence). The description of the American Revolution in the second lesson described the colonists' victory over Britain even as they had fewer numbers of soldiers and supplies, and briefly described the help from the European countries of Spain and France. The third lesson described the deliberative process of setting up a new government in a fledgling country, with explicit attention to the ways in which the framers of the Constitution sought compromise. The fourth and final lesson of the unit described the efforts of the young United States to explore (Lewis and Clark's expeditions) and to establish itself on the world stage, identifying boundaries and policies concerning its relationship to other countries.

6 • LEARNING TO HIDE

The next unit explored the "westward expansion" of the United States and briefly discussed the ways in which the technologies of the time facilitated this movement. The second lesson explored how Andrew Jackson prompted the establishment of the Democratic Party and described his presidency as oriented toward "the common man" (Duran et al., 2005, p. 118), but dismissively described the forced relocation of Native Americans (i.e., the Trail of Tears) under Jackson's direction as "Moving the Native Americans" (p. 122)—ignoring its own hazardous implication that Native Americans were separate from "the common man." The period of the mid-1800s was explored in the third lesson and included information about industrial expansion and the wave of European immigration that expansion prompted, as well as a brief description of the beginnings of the women's suffrage movement.

Unit Four explored how Texas and California came to be new states in the young nation, noting, "A war with Mexico gave land to the United States" (Duran et al., 2005, p. 139), but Mexico's prohibition of slavery and the US's provocative placement of troops next to the Rio Grande River (instead of the more commonly accepted border of the Nueces River, which was further north) were not explored as precipitating factors. The next lesson described how slavery became a divisive issue for the United States, with the North wishing to outlaw slavery and the South wishing to preserve it in the interest of states' rights. The Civil War was the topic of the third lesson of the unit, which briefly included attention to the significant battles during the war and Lincoln's eventual signing of the Emancipation Proclamation to lead to the end of the war. There was no mention of Juneteenth, the day on which the last people enslaved in Texas were emancipated, and a day which President Biden declared a federal holiday in 2021. Lincoln's 1862 directive to hang 38 Dakota tribal members found guilty of participating in the U.S.-Dakota War was omitted as well.

The time period between 1865 and 1914 was the focus of Unit Five. The first lesson of the unit described Reconstruction, the process of integrating the South back into the nation, as well as the 13th, 14th, and 15th Amendments to the Constitution and the challenges prompted by Lincoln's assassination. There was no mention of the New Jim Crow laws that essentially ended Reconstruction or the ways in which previously enslaved Black people were systemically disenfranchised and criminalized by these laws. The second lesson focused on the next wave of immigrants who arrived in the U.S. from Northern Europe. The third lesson, "Becoming a World Power," described the U.S.'s victory in the Spanish-American War, as well as Hawaii's eventual statehood. In neither this unit, nor the previous one (where the incorporation of Texas and California were discussed and the Monroe Doctrine could have been) did the textbook make any linkage between U.S. expansion (or imperialism) and the presence of Latinx populations in the United States.

Unit Six included just two lessons but spanned the years between 1914 and 1945. The unit included in the first lesson a discussion of World War I, the "Roaring Twenties," the Great Depression, and President Roosevelt's "New Deal." There were references to the work of white women who worked for women's suffrage, but no suffragists of color were mentioned here or in earlier units (i.e., wherein Sojourner Truth's and others' contributions might have been highlighted). The second lesson described World War II and explained the many fronts of the war in Europe, the Pacific, and the ways in which the war influenced life in the mainland United States.

Unit Seven covered the Cold War, including a brief discussion of communism in the Soviet Union and the effects of the Cold War in the United States. The second lesson superficially explored racial prejudice—oddly the first point at which race was explicitly discussed as a cause of conflict in the U.S. (excepting the four paragraphs noted earlier about slavery and abolitionism and states' rights to decide on these matters as precipitators of the Civil War)—and described the Civil Rights Movement and how the African American struggle for equality prompted other historically marginalized groups (e.g., women, Mexican Americans) to fight for equality as well. There was no mention of the role of the Black Panthers in policing the police, or of Dolores Huerta and César Chávez and their fight for migrant workers' rights. The third lesson of the unit explored the time from the 1990s forward, exploring the new world powers and "threats to world peace" (Duran et al., 2005, p. 262). Important prospective connections to the United States' role in destabilizing the countries in Central America—e.g., Guatemala's CIA-backed 1954 coup and decades of subsequent violence and subordination of the indigenous population, support for the Contras against Nicaragua's popular but Marxist-leaning Sandinistas), and support for right-wing 'anti-communist' forces in El Salvador's 1980s Civil War—and that history's relevance for prompting immigration to the United States from these countries were completely omitted.

The eighth unit of the *Access* textbook was entitled, "Civics in America," and its first lesson described the United States Constitution and the three branches of the government. The next lesson described the Bill of Rights and the rights and freedoms these amendments guarantee; Mrs. Durham had previously included this information in the second unit in which students learned about the establishment of the Constitution. The third and final lesson discussed "Responsible Citizenship," including the rights and responsibilities fundamental to United States citizenship. There was no nuanced discussion of the notion of citizenship as a practice as distinguished from immigration status, ignoring the ways in which these two ideas have been conflated.

During my fieldwork, the students explored Units Two, Three, and Four, and Mrs. Durham supplemented this curriculum with a two-week-long unit she had designed on U.S. elections in the weeks leading up to the 2016 general election. This unit included a description of the Democratic and Republican political parties in the U.S., as well as the candidates from each of these parties who were running for President of the United States. Students explored election issues through the ISideWith.com website to understand how their stances aligned with the dif-

8 • LEARNING TO HIDE

ferent candidates; notably, this website included all candidates for president, including those from third parties.

THE CLASS ROUTINE

The students in Mrs. Durham's classroom learned and enacted a number of routines throughout their day at school. Since they started the day in Mrs. Durham's class, I arrived most mornings to find students lining the walls of the hallway outside of their classroom—congregated in small groups—chatting quietly or reading while they waited for Mrs. Durham or Mrs. Sánchez to arrive and unlock the classroom door. I often sat alongside them on the cold tiled floor, leaning back on the red brick walls. There were some mornings when I sat with them to help with homework, and other mornings when I exchanged greetings in Spanish and then sat quietly with them.

The class routine unfolded predictably most days. While some mornings the room took on a mellow and calm atmosphere, on other mornings the room buzzed with adolescent energy. Mrs. Durham usually arrived before Mrs. Sánchez—her arms loaded with bags and supplies—and the group of students closest to the door scurried around her to lift the bags from her shoulders and to help her unlock the door. Once the door was opened, students flooded into the room and scattered into desks and chairs or sank into the small sofa. Mrs. Durham and usually Alejandro would begin plugging in lamps and string lights around the room. When those were all illuminated, Mrs. Durham would turn off the overhead light and sigh, "Aah."

The room was normally full of kids in the morning, often with over 30 of them milling around before classes started. It was usually quite noisy with lots of boisterous and excited chatter. Boys greeted each other by slapping hands and exchanging handshakes. The girls sat with their smart phones, gathered in a circle. They talked about soccer, each other, other girls, or boys. Some pretended to fight, and many conversed in their indigenous languages from Guatemala (i.e., Mam, Q'anjob'al, and K'iche'). When the warning bell signaled two minutes before the start of classes, half of the students in the classroom filtered out of the classroom and headed across the hall to Mrs. Burton's classroom where they alternated between ELA class and science class. Students settled into the day slowly, sharpening pencils and running back to their lockers for a pencil or notebook. Mrs. Durham and Mrs. Sánchez typically settled in slowly as well, checking in with each other and with students.

The first block class formally started each morning with Mrs. Durham offering a "Good morning," as she surveyed the 16 students' moods and body language from her chair behind her desk. She called the students' names as she documented attendance at her computer. Students responded to their names with "here" or "sí," sometimes answering "no here" when they noticed a classmate's absence. When Mrs. Durham finished calling attendance, she prompted them to get out their notebooks to start on their "bell ringers." Bell ringers were short warm-up activities

The Political Work of the ELL Program at WRHS • 9

that usually consisted of a few written questions that were projected on the front board and aimed to review the previous history lesson's material. Students had a few minutes to write responses to the questions before Mrs. Durham asked for volunteers to share their answers with the class. A handful of students volunteered their responses by raising their hands and waiting for Mrs. Durham to call on them. As students shared what they had written, other students copied down the answers or made corrections to what they had already written.

Following the bell ringer, students opened their textbooks to the specified page, usually pausing to joke and chuckle about Mrs. Durham's (mis)pronunciation of the Spanish word, "página *(page)*." This normally meant mimicking her pronunciation—in which she regularly placed the spoken emphasis on the wrong syllable—or making attempts to pronounce it incorrectly in a different way. This never seemed to get old for the students, and Mrs. Durham laughed along with them, practicing the correct pronunciation they modeled for her. (I never clarified whether her mispronunciations became intentional to create this enduring ritual.)

The remainder of the lesson almost always proceeded in the same way: Mrs. Durham would read a few sentences from the textbook and then pause for Mrs. Sánchez to translate the sentences to Spanish. (When Mrs. Sánchez was absent, Alejandro, a student who was proficient in Spanish and English, translated during first block unless the other bilingual paraeducator was free to help in the class. A formally designated student assistant[4] sometimes helped translate during second block in this situation.) Then Mrs. Durham would read the remainder of the paragraph or page, and Mrs. Sánchez would again translate. Most students appeared to follow along with the reading (which was only the English language textbook) and would then look up toward Mrs. Sánchez as she translated. Mrs. Durham would then project a slide, which inevitably made students groan, and several students predictably asked, "Copy?" Mrs. Durham would affirmatively answer "Sí," consistently each time they asked, and then the students' bent their heads over their notebooks as they wrote.

After they had made their way through the reading and notes for the day, Mrs. Durham would distribute a textbook supplement worksheet, and the students would groan in ritual protest. The worksheets, adapted for sheltered instruction (i.e., shorter questions, simplified wording, etc.), reviewed the highlighted vocabulary and concepts from the reading and notes. Students often worked in small groups, turning toward one another in their desks; they were also often allowed to use their phones to listen to music as they worked. Most of them listened to Spanish-language music in a range of genres. When the bell signaled the end of

---

[4] Student assistants were enrolled in a course called "School to Career," in which they were paired with professionals in careers in which they were interested. While students could seek out opportunities of interest to them (subject to the school's approval), the student assistants in Mrs. Durham's classroom were encouraged to participate in the ELL classrooms because of their bilingualism; in many cases, the student assistants elected to serve in Mrs. Durham's classroom more because they enjoyed being in the classroom more than having a professional interest in the work.

10 • LEARNING TO HIDE

class, students scrambled to gather their books and other materials and rushed into the hallway to chat with friends or to visit the restroom. Students rarely ventured out of their immediate 'ELL hallway', instead leaning against the walls or their lockers and chatting.

The second block was similar in size to the first block with 22 students, but most students arrived in the classroom with plenty of time before the bell since they were just coming from the classroom across the hall. This class followed a similar routine to the first block class's, except for the time right after the bell signaling the beginning of class. As soon as the bell sounded, the intercom beeped, and the students stood upon hearing it. "Good morning, Washington River High!" exclaimed a boisterous male student voice (the same student representative from the Student Council) from the speaker on the wall. All the students in the classroom stood to face the flag hanging above the door, and the speaker continued, "Please join me in reciting the 'Pledge of Allegiance'." Some students mumbled a few words of the Pledge, mostly the ends of the lines. Mostly, though, it was quiet in the room (not in defiance of the Pledge so much as unfamiliarity and little participation by peers). At the conclusion of the Pledge, the speaker said, "Thank you. And now for your announcements."

That was the cue for ELL students to tune out and resume their conversations, and most of them began to chat with classmates around them. The announcements, all in English, sometimes lasted for as long as five minutes. This routine was familiar from my own world language classroom in this same school, but I recalled that the students in my classroom (typically monolingual English speakers learning Spanish as a new language) spoke the words of the Pledge in monotone and were mostly quiet throughout the announcements, often asking me follow-up questions to clarify dates, times, or locations of announced events. The ritual of reciting the "Pledge of Allegiance" in the ELL classroom was always a moment that gave me pause because while the students stood respectfully and some even attempted to recite the words intermittently, it struck me that they received daily messages in the media and in their daily lives (see, for example, earlier discussion of Donald Trump's language describing immigrants) that conveyed unwelcome and discrimination.

At the conclusion of the announcements, second block proceeded almost exactly as the first block, with the same lesson and generally the same schedule following the attendance roll call. The main difference between the two classes was that the students in the second class were much more energetic and gregarious in general; this may have been because they had had time to wake up their teenage brains or simply because of the mix of personalities in the classes.

POLICIES AND PRACTICES REFLECT VALUES

As I stated at the beginning of this chapter, policies and practices reflect values, explicitly and implicitly. What do the policies and practices of WRHS say about the values of the school and the community? As the ample literature on language planning explores (e.g., Bacon, 2018; Matias, 2016; Tollefson, 1991), ignoring students' multilingual proficiencies in languages other than English reveals ideologies of English as the dominant language and perpetuating white supremacy. Indeed, bilingualism and bilingual education are political issues that are often veiled in the ideological cloaks of benevolent racism (López & Velásquez, 2006; Peralta, 2013; Hamann, 2002) and conservatives' romantic assimilationist notions of a country united by their belief in English as the dominant language (Cervantes-Soon, 2014). In turn, simplistic and monolithic expectations for U.S. history learning reveal conservative notions of one America told through majoritarian stories (e.g., Love, 2004; Mitchell, 2013)—e.g., "the land of the free and the home of the brave." Furthermore, WRHS's graduation requirements were created with a specific student in mind—a student who had entered school in the district (or at least in the state) in kindergarten and progressed successfully through the standardized curriculum of the school through instruction in English. Students are held to a standard of sameness regardless of their life experiences, revealing the conservative rhetoric of self-reliance (Apple, 2004, 2014). But what happens when a student with limited or interrupted formal schooling enters high school at age 15 or age 18? They face a very real challenge in being able to finish all the requirements by the maximum enrollment age allowed by state law (i.e., 21), especially if they are expected to learn English *before* earning credits for other classes. The students at WRHS were earning credits for core classes in a sheltered format, but the curriculum was less than robust and dismissive of students' funds of knowledge (Gonzalez et al., 2005; Moll et al., 1992) and segregated students based on a deficiency in English (Jaffe-Walter & Miranda, 2020; Valdés, 2001; Valenzuela, 1999).

The "official curriculum" (i.e., the written standards and objectives) (Posner, 2004) of United States history for newcomers at WRHS, presented superficially and chronologically, framed a survey-style course in which topics were regarded as static and disconnected from the present, including the flow of circumstances that had brought these learners to this very classroom and their families to Washington River. Moreover, the topics that were included represented only a sliver of the history of the United States—an overwhelmingly *safe* history. There was no space for a critical analysis of the connections between, for example, the U.S. military interventions in and economic policies relating to Mexico and Central America and the resulting push factors prompting immigration from those areas to the U.S. Relying on the monolithic curriculum of the *Access* textbook meant that learning United States history was reduced to memorizing a set of whitewashed facts about the safe heroes doing the winning. This conception of U.S. history manifests notions of empire, American Exceptionalism, and settler colonialism.

Even when Mrs. Durham presented the students with an opportunity to learn about political parties and voting in the United States, there was only one student in the class who would be eligible to vote—in the 2016 general election or thereafter. Certainly all students—regardless of eligibility to vote—should understand the structures, processes, and ideologies at play in the politics of the United States. However, is it especially important that small 'c' citizens have opportunities to learn about, reimagine, and plan ways that they, too, can assert agency in the public space.

Curriculum, though, is always planned and mediated by the teacher and taken up by students in response to lived experience. Pedagogies, understood as the project of teaching and learning, offer an opportunity to complicate and transform the curriculum and to position learners in it. The predictable scripts that guided the daily routine in this classroom and school neglected these opportunities, perhaps in part because Mrs. Durham's qualification to lead this class was based on her ESL language teaching certification rather than preparation as a secondary social studies teacher.

It is through the persistent and insistent interrogation of curriculum that learners claim membership and belonging in it. Marching through and perpetuating a monolithic curriculum of majoritarian stories dismisses the realities of the learners in the room and is a demonstration of what Kara Viesca and I (2021) have called "evasion pedagogy"—willfully *evading* opportunities for addressing inequities in school and in society.

The official curriculum (Posner, 2004), while an important frame for the activity in this classroom, became background during my observations of the life of the classroom. However, the "hidden curriculum" (Jackson, 1968)—what students were actually positioned to learn irrespective of formally declared learning goals and situated in the quotidian life of the classroom—and the pedagogies enacted by the teachers *and* students provided a window into the ways students constructed citizenship in this space, which I take up in the next chapter.

CHAPTER 2

THE PEOPLE IN THE CLASSROOM

Each of the people in Mrs. Durham's ELL classroom at WRHS brought unique intersectional identities to their shared space. Their racial, linguistic, classed, and gendered biographies shaped how they saw and experienced the world, and thus, how they constructed and modeled citizen identities. The students, despite sharing many similarities in age and life experiences, were a diverse group of individuals. The unique perspectives, experiences, and power of the teacher, Mrs. Durham, influenced the life of the classroom substantially. Mrs. Sánchez, too, held a position of power as a paraeducator in the classroom, and the students regarded her as *maestra* (teacher) even as the school district did not quite. The hierarchy of institutional stratification, however, also positioned her as an assistant to the teacher, which meant that Mrs. Durham delegated clerical tasks to her.

THE STUDENTS

The students in this classroom were a vibrant mix of backgrounds and personalities. Some days, they shuffled quietly and slowly into the classroom, shoulders drooping; other days, they exuded boundless energy that reverberated throughout the room. The students made this classroom theirs, and they welcomed new-

Learning to Hide: The English Learning Classroom as Sanctuary and Trap
pages 13–27.
Copyright © 2024 by Information Age Publishing
www.infoagepub.com
All rights of reproduction in any form reserved.

14 • LEARNING TO HIDE

comers into their community, serving as ambassadors by showing them the ropes and fostering belonging in the classroom and cafeteria. While the students were teenagers and demonstrated typical characteristics of adolescence, like impulsivity, independence, and dependence, they simultaneously demonstrated strength, resilience, and perseverance as they encountered their new realities in their new school—many of them after having made stressful and dangerous journeys to the United States.

The students in this classroom ranged in age from 15 years old to 19 years. They wore many of the outward symbols of the all-American teen of 2016: acid-washed skinny jeans, Converse low-top sneakers scuffed just enough but not too much, track pants, and white Reebok sneakers reminiscent of the style of the 1980s. Most of the girls wore their long dark hair piled on top of their heads in a messy bun or slicked back into a tight ponytail. The boys sported short-cropped hairstyles ranging from sleek and styled to purposefully mussed. One particularly stylish young man, Armando, wore combat boots most days with his skinny jeans, his patterned shirt buttoned all the way to the top. His hair was always perfectly coiffed, and he often helped style his peers' shirts in just the right balance between tucked-in and untucked; a heavy waft of strong musky cologne preceded his entrance into the classroom and immediately permeated all corners of the room. Most of the girls wore meticulously applied make-up each day, highlighting their eyes and framing their lips. Yet despite their wardrobe and coiffing similarities, their stories were as diverse as their personalities, and each of them had experienced immigration, migration, and life in general uniquely.

Out of the 38 students between the first and second block classes, seven students from this classroom participated in in-depth interviews with me. These seven students came to Washington River from Mexico, Guatemala, El Salvador, Costa Rica, and Honduras. In all but one case (Alejandro's), students explained that they came to the United States to escape the economic challenges and safety concerns in their home countries. The length of time they had lived in the U.S. was between three and fifteen months, so only one (Isabel) of them had prior experience in Washington River's middle or elementary schools. The students brought to their shared classroom different personalities and life experiences, diverse journeys they took to get to the U.S., and unique dispositions toward and before their schooling experience in Washington River. Below, I offer brief introductions to the seven students who I interviewed to illustrate the diversity of their experiences.

Diverse Life Experiences of Students

Anyelín was reserved and softspoken, and at 17 years old, she had been in the United States for fifteen months when I met her. She was from a village in the western highlands of Guatemala, a region speckled with small villages and bordering the Mexican state of Chiapas. She entered the room quietly each morning, her big brown eyes downcast, and rested her head on her arms atop her desk until

The People in the Classroom • **15**

class started or a classmate came to talk with her. She worked at McDonald's after school most days, and she expressed her frustration and urgency to learn English, which she felt would make her work more manageable.

Saraí was also from the western highlands of Guatemala, but where Anyelín had lived in a smaller village, Saraí had lived in a city for most of her fifteen years before coming to the United States in September of 2016. Her bright red lipstick outlined her words and illuminated her ever-present smile, and she tossed her long black hair playfully over her shoulder as she chatted with friends. She enjoyed being a teenager, explaining that had she stayed in Guatemala, she already would have been training to be a nurse.

Sayra, nearing 19 years of age at the time of the study, was the oldest student in the class and was from a city in the Mexican state of Guanajuato. She had been living in Washington River for close to a year when I met her. Her dark eyes sparkled and her wide smile beamed as she reminisced about walking the plazas as a little girl with her grandmother. Sayra knew that her father's work in the United States was more stable than it had been in Mexico, but she hoped to eventually return to Mexico.

Jesús was from a city in central Mexico as well, and at 16 years old, had been living in Washington River for approximately eight months. He and his family had moved to the Midwest after a short time in New York. I often saw Jesús extending kindness to his classmates—sharing his bag full of grapes or offering a handful of chips. He attributed his kindness to Christian teachings he learned at church. Jesús was affected by Cerebral Palsy and he walked with a slight limp. He was often the first to volunteer when Mrs. Durham sought a "big strong man" to help move a piece of furniture or unload the boxes of soda from her car. He joked with other students that he was stronger and more handsome than they were, proudly flexing his arms to show off his muscles, his eyes twinkling with his smile.

Isabel was a personable student with a ready smile and laugh. She was a close friend of Sayra, and they always sat together in Mrs. Durham's class. She, like Sayra, enjoyed having friends in her classes, admitting with a giggle that she really loved her classes with Mrs. Durham "porque tengo a todos mis amigos. *(Because I have all my friends in there.)."* Isabel's bubbly personality was magnetic, and she was rarely alone. Isabel was 15 years old when I met her, having come from a small village in El Salvador. She had lived with her grandparents there, her mother having left for the United States when Isabel was only a month old. She had corresponded with her mother with an occasional card or letter until her parents felt that she and her sister were old enough to make the trip to the United States.

Alejandro was a gregarious 15-year-old from a city in central Costa Rica with a wide, sparkly smile, dark brown eyes, and sleekly styled black hair. Alejandro was exceedingly likeable, and students and teachers were quick to forgive him his moments of occasional disrespect. He was unique in this class for a variety of reasons: 1) he spoke English very well and often translated for Mrs. Durham

16 • LEARNING TO HIDE

when Mrs. Sánchez was absent or out of the classroom, 2) he was a voluntary migrant, having come to Washington River to stay with an aunt and uncle as a sort of study abroad experience, and 3) he participated in the boys' basketball and track teams. His facility with English (learned in school in Costa Rica) afforded him the respect of his peers in the class, as they saw him as more intelligent because he could quickly answer questions and translate for them. His English proficiency allowed him to participate more fully in extra-curricular activities and interact with non-ELL teammates on a regular basis, an experience most of his peers in the ELL classes did not share. His placement in the newcomer ELL classes was curious, given his high proficiency in English.

Caterín Michelle, with her large brown eyes and tight-spiraled curls of long black hair, was—at 18 years old—a motherly figure in the class. She spoke fondly about her classmates as she alluded to their shared experiences in school. Caterín Michelle was from Honduras and had been in the U.S. for six months at the time I met her. Her mother had been living in Washington River for three years before Caterín Michelle and her three siblings arrived. Caterín Michelle found Washington River to be quite different from her life in Honduras. Gangs and gang activity had often dictated where and when she could leave her home or even go to school; indeed, this violence was the main reason they left Honduras.

These seven students shared a variety of common experiences in their backgrounds. They shared a sense of urgency in learning English, and for most of them, their journeys to the United States involved a significant amount of time apart from their parents—with their parents and/or older siblings traveling to the U.S. before them (in a phenomenon known as "chain migration" [Boyd, 1989; Haug, 2008]). Economic challenges in their home countries prompted most of them to come to the U.S. While their journeys were surely unique, they had in common the traumatic experience of leaving what they knew to start a new life in an unfamiliar place. Finally, they were similar in their aspirations for their futures. Almost all of the students indicated that graduation from high school followed by a well-paying steady job would be an important achievement in their futures so that they would be able to take care of their parents. College was a goal that most of them seemed to think was out of their reach, mainly for financial reasons (although Nebraska does offer in-state tuition to all who graduate from a high school within the state).

While there were several similarities in the students' life experiences, there were some interesting differences as well. For example, the older students—Anyelín (17), Sayra (18), and Caterín Michelle (18)—all talked about their desire to graduate and to get on to working to help take care of their families. Their primary concern was being able to stay in school long enough to learn English. The younger students, in contrast, did not seem to feel this same pressure of time.

Anyelín was unique in this subset of the class in that she had a job outside of school. However, this was typical of the rest of the students in the classroom—most students worked between 30–50 hours each week. She worked between five and six hours each day after school, and she insisted that the work was manage-able with her school schedule. Mrs. Durham and Mrs. Sánchez kept close track of how much students were working, knowing that some of the employers had a reputation for requiring their young workers to stay extra hours. Mrs. Durham and Mrs. Sánchez assisted working students with earning credits for work experience, which was productive in accumulating elective credits toward graduation. How-ever, many students (although only one who participated in my study) in the ELL program worked long overnight hours and were visibly tired and sometimes still dirty from their shifts that may have ended only a couple of hours before the start of school. In these cases, students slept after school until their shifts started, and this left little time for completing homework or making up missed schoolwork from absences, not to mention limiting opportunities to participate in after-school activities. Working students often struggled to stay awake during class, especially during sessions in which they took notes for long stretches of time.

The Commonalities in Their Experiences

Newcomers face a number of challenges in their experiences of life and school, considering the enduring stressors associated with migration (see, for example, Bal & Perzigian, 2013; Hilburn, 2014). Newcomers, especially young migrants, in NLD contexts likely experience stressors from leaving a familiar environment combined with their immersion in a new culture and language. The students with whom I spoke in Mrs. Durham's classroom, having come from the Northern Triangle countries of Honduras, El Salvador, and Guatemala, also described the trauma resulting from political, economic, and social burdens, such as extended separation from family members, living and traveling alone, and the day-to-day stress of securing personal safety in their home countries. Certainly, immigrants arrive in the U.S. for a whole host of reasons, but the similarities in the harrowing experiences of the students in this class were notable.

The students in this classroom, as diverse as they were, shared the status of being adolescents, exhibiting typical teenager behaviors, like expressing their identities through fashion, humor, and impulsivity (Becker, 1990), and compet-ing with one another for the best grades or social popularity. However, they also shared the experience of being new and all that being new entailed. They agonized with each other over the urgency and difficulty of learning English, and they eas-ily identified with the disorientation they saw many of their peers experience upon arrival in WRHS.

Being Teens Together

Most of the students—indeed, all those who I interviewed—spoke about their peers fondly. Caterín Michelle said with a soft smile, "He llegado a quererlos porque se dan el querer *(I've learned to love them because they show me love)*." This love she spoke of grew out of their shared experience of being new and being in this classroom together. She explained, "Algo que no entiendo ellos me ayudan a que le entienda *(Something that I don't know they help me to understand).*" Their friendships and fondness for one another also manifested in a typically adolescent way; Caterín Michelle laughed, "They're always bothering me in a way that they bother me, but not in a bad way." I could see this in the ways many of them pretended to steal another's seat or phone or teasingly tug on a strand of hair of the person seated in front of them, sometimes even poking him or her in the side to see him or her jump in surprise.

Another part of their classroom life that resonated with my own experience of having taught high school students was the pervasiveness and intensity of competition among them. The students' competitiveness also influenced how Mrs. Durham planned her lessons. When we talked one morning about alternate ideas for test review, she acknowledged that the review guide was mundane and routine. However, she noted that while she was familiar with several games they could play to review course material, she found that the students with higher levels of English proficiency always had an edge over students who needed more time to understand the English in order to answer a question about content. Competition turned bitter, in her experience, because games revealed the differences in English proficiency too markedly. Because Mrs. Durham wanted to maintain a supportive and collaborative environment in her classroom and in the ELL program, she aimed to diminish competition over academic achievement. We never discussed the prospect of game designs that did not stratify students by English proficiency.

Other sure markers of adolescence were the loquacious Monday morning conversations about what they had done over the weekend. Perhaps because of work schedules as well as family responsibilities, few of them saw each other outside of school, so they were eager to catch up with one another after two days apart. On these days, students gathered in groups and chatted happily. For example, two boys sat talking quietly in adjacent rocking chairs, which they had moved closer together. Ignoring the giggling and chatting elsewhere in the room, they talked about who had been seen with whom over the weekend and discussed the food they had at family gatherings. Students were almost always in good spirits on Mondays, which contrasted with the slumped shoulders and frowns I remembered on Mondays from when I was a high school teacher (albeit a high school teacher of native English-speaking students who often had spent their whole life in the community).

Being New

While students faced the everyday challenges that come with being a teen, they also faced substantial challenges stemming from the fact that they were newcomers to Washington River and—in the case of most students—to the United States. "Being new" was an experience students shared, and this experience influenced the ways in which they constructed their daily lives.

The experience of being new to Washington River and to the U.S. meant that *so much* was new and different. For example, immunizations were required, but school uniforms were not. They used lockers to store their personal belongings, which involved learning to open the locker with a combination lock. They had to learn their lunch code and to navigate the lunch routine in the cafeteria. They needed to complete and submit paperwork for free and reduced-price lunches and numerous other enrollment forms. Some students were even attending school for the first time or for the first time in many years. As if this long list of "newness" was not enough, students were encountering each day in English, a language that was brand new to most of them. Alejandro—even with his well-developed English proficiency—remembered the feelings of alienation he felt when he was new to Washington River, writing, "Cuando recién llegué aquí todo era extraño. Las personas hablaban extraño, las escuelas de aquí tienes que usar loker y no ropa de uniforme *(When I first arrived here recently, everything was strange. The people spoke strangely, the schools here—you have to use lockers and there's no uniform.).*" For him, entering the new school brought a number of changes and unfamiliar routines.

Caterín Michelle, remembering her first days at WRHS, said that although the experience of being new was lonely and strange, she appreciated the help of the students and teachers—Mrs. Sánchez included—in making the transition. "Llegué y vi que ellos—los otros compañeros—se hablaban con confianza *(I arrived and I saw that they all my other classmates would talk to each other with a lot of confidence in each other.).*"

Anyelín admitted that it was daunting at first to imagine herself fitting into this tightly-knit community, but she noted that new students should not worry—that others were there to help them. She offered advice to new students who may feel isolated or anxious about being new: "Que no se sentiría mal, que aquí estamos nosotros para ayudarlos, que acepta ayuda *(To not feel bad, that we are here to help him or her, they should accept help.).*" She acknowledged the important role current students served in helping new students learn to do school at WRHS. It is striking to note that in this construct of 'new' various 'current' students who had been at WRHS only a few months or just over a year saw themselves as hosts helping those who were yet 'newer' to Washington River.

Saraí recalled that she felt nervous and strange as a new student; her first day at lunch was when other students started talking to her and that helped her feel less isolated. Sayra, too, pointed to lunchtime as an important social time to get to

20 • LEARNING TO HIDE

know each other. She said, "Al principio me sentí extraña porque todo fue diferente *(At first I felt strange because everything was different.)*." However, when lunchtime rolled around, one of her classmates raised her hand and waved at her from a table in the cafeteria, motioning for her to join them. This, she said, was when she began to feel accepted.

Caterín Michelle acknowledged that it just took time to get to know each other: "Me sentía nerviosa, pero poco a poco fui hablándoles, y ya somos amigos. Y no para de molestar *(I felt nervous, but little by little I started talking to them, and now we're friends. And they don't stop bugging me.).*" She laughed and rolled her eyes as she recounted how Diego would steal her seat or snatch her pencil from her desk when she was not looking.

New students were also in the position of having to trust others. They had to divulge a substantial amount of personal information to be enrolled. Since many of the new students wished to hold jobs and earn graduation credits from their work, many of them entrusted Mrs. Durham and Mrs. Sánchez with the names under which they worked; these names were often not their given names. They trusted that their teachers would not betray this information. They were likewise in the position to have to trust the translators when they visited the nurse, their guidance counselor, or the main office.

Teasing and Humor

Teasing and humor were important parts of the students' classroom lives. They delighted in a well-timed joke or one-liner, and they found a wide range of topics to be worth a laugh—even if sometimes it approached 'gallows humor' (i.e., laughing at the painful and difficult). Alejandro took particular pleasure in performing imitations, often entering the room with a smirk, and saying to Mrs. Durham in a perfect impression of the school's principal, "Morning," his voice deep and resonating. His prank worked every time, with Mrs. Durham responding with wide eyes in disbelief at the likeness of the impression and Alejandro throwing his head back as he grinned.

There were also instances of wry humor that bespoke the students' observations of the world around them. In one such instance, the morning announcements had seemed to go on for much longer than usual—in English and thus incomprehensible to most of them. When they finally came to an end, Diego dramatically looked around and pointed up at the intercom device on the wall, tilted his head, and asked with feigned seriousness, "¿Qué dijo *(What did he say)*?" Everyone giggled and chuckled, and I could not stifle a smile myself as I realized his question was a sarcastic rhetorical nod to the fact that the school's announcements were not accessible to them.

Other times, there were jokes that prompted a sad laugh; the content of the joke was funny only because it made light of their realities. For example, when Jorge made a joke about the wall Donald Trump promised to build on the southern U.S. border with Mexico—"They gotta deport immigrants so they can help build the

The People in the Classroom • **21**

wall in Mexico"—students laughed. Mrs. Durham lamented, "Only in this room can you laugh about issues like this." Observing this interaction, I wrote in my fieldnotes, *"This makes me so sad. It's funny (?), but it's so not funny."*

The election and the prospects of their lives in a Trump presidency served as material for sarcasm and moments of levity. As noted in the Preface, Mrs. Durham attempted to reassure students the morning following the election that they would be safe in the United States in a Trump administration. After some serious words about how he did not have all the power just because he was president, she paused and said with a grin, "I don't have a very large basement...but I do have a basement. You can come live with me." Mrs. Sánchez translated, with a smirk on her face, and when she finished speaking, students giggled and looked around at each other. This idea of Mrs. Durham's basement as a refuge for them was recurrent that day and in the days and weeks following. Later that same morning, Alejandro looked around the room and asked where Mrs. Sánchez went, and Mrs. Durham explained that she was in the office registering another new student. He responded with mock seriousness, "God, Mrs. Durham, your basement really is gonna get full." Students around him smiled and giggled.

Weeks later, just after students had returned from a long Thanksgiving weekend, students worked quietly in groups, chatting as they completed a worksheet. One student periodically broke out into loud song, and Mrs. Durham gave him an admonishing look to quiet him the first few times. When he started to belt out the song's chorus one more time, Mrs. Durham looked at him seriously and said, "If you sing like that, you're not moving into my basement." Students—including the singer—laughed at the reference to her basement and at the implication that the quality of his singing would prohibit him from gaining refuge there. These moments of levity were means of negotiating an unfolding volatile political spectacle—one over which they had no influence or control.

The range of things that students teased each other about was wide and diverse. There was a pattern of teasing involved in their note-taking routine in which someone would yell, "Next!" seconds after Mrs. Durham projected a slide for them to copy. Predictably, most students would protest, retorting, "No!" or "Digo, hol' on *(Hold on).*" No matter how many times they enacted this routine, Mrs. Durham ignored them and kept the slide projected. Students also teased each other about their English proficiency, especially when a substitute teacher asked them to read aloud. The differences in proficiency remained an awkward subject. While students like Alejandro—whose pronunciation, fluency, and comprehension were quite developed—read loudly and confidently, other students who had less time learning English were teased for their quiet voices as they stumbled through the passages. They seemed to take this teasing in stride, but the language teacher in me wanted so badly to protectively intervene; language learning, especially in adolescence, is such a vulnerable experience and the stakes for learning English were so high.

22 • LEARNING TO HIDE

As widely diverse as their experiences were, the newcomers in this classroom shared the experience of being new. This shared experience of being new bonded them as they made sense of new lives and constructed new hybrid identities in their ELL classroom together (Irizarry, 2007). The ELL classroom was a space where their shared familiarity with Spanish allowed them to rely on their more developed linguistic skills to communicate with each other. In Spanish, they could joke with and tease each other, and also argue, but in English, those interpersonal moments were much more strained and limited.

Mrs. Durham, their teacher, and Mrs. Sánchez, who they also called *maestra,* played important roles in fostering the kind of familial environment in which they could openly share, ask questions, and guide one another. I should add that *maestro* and *maestra,* the masculine and feminine terms for teacher in Spanish are more than just translations of a kind of job. Throughout Latin America each are used as honorifics, terms used to indicate respect akin to how 'doctor' is sometimes used in American English. Referencing Mrs. Durham as *maestra* indicated reverence for her role. That the paraeducator, Mrs. Sánchez, was recognized with the same honorific highlighted that, to students, her role seemed no less elevated and prestigious than Mrs. Durham's.

MRS. DURHAM: THE TEACHER

The official teacher in the classroom, Mrs. Durham, sat with me in her empty classroom on a wintry mid-December afternoon, having just finished cleaning up the last vestiges of a holiday party for the students. She leaned back in her chair with a soft smile spread across her face as our conversation began. I asked, "What do you wish people knew about your students?" She paused thoughtfully, looking down at her desk, and sighed:

> I think they're the bravest human beings I know. People think they just came here because they want a better life, but it's more than just a better life. I mean, people think 'better life'—yeah, that means more money or better living conditions, but it's so much more than that for them. It is money for them, for their family back home who may not have a reliable source of income every day…so that somebody in their family back home is eating. So they can have an education, that they actually finish or go through 'cause so many of them are coming in with limited formal education. It's not just, you know, yeah, better life, but it's so much more than that…and they're *so* brave. They have gone through and seen more things than any person in their entire lifetime should, and at a young age. They're the most amazing human beings. They make me a better person every day.

Mrs. Durham put her whole self into her work at WRHS. When students entered her classroom, they became a part of the "family tree" within the room— an intricate web of relationships that spanned states and countries. Having been employed at WRHS for ten years—thus with an initial tenure that overlapped

The People in the Classroom • **23**

my time as a Spanish teacher there—Mrs. Durham was the thread that wove the relationships together.

She was a 30-something white woman whose dominant language was English and, having grown up in a nearby community, she was familiar with the culture and history of Washington River. She spoke often about her young child, and she enjoyed showing pictures and recounting stories about him to her students. Mrs. Durham's students seemed to enjoy her spunk and occasionally sassy nature. Her short gold-streaked hair framed her face, and her eyes were always moving—sometimes in thoughtful concentration and other times in twinkling laughter. She delighted in getting to know her students and she greatly enjoyed gently teasing them.

By disposition and necessity a multi-tasker, she scurried about the classroom, managing the needs of different groups of students and keeping a lesson moving while at the same time making a cup of coffee. One morning, while the students were working on a review guide for their upcoming test, Mrs. Durham made a phone call to inquire about health insurance for a former student. At the same time, two students entered from another class to take a test in her room, and she got them settled and reminded them that they were not allowed to use notes. She went back to her desk—stopping beside a student's desk to answer a question—and made another call to fix a student's birth certificate because the mom's name was not on it.

Mrs. Durham influenced the construction of citizenship within this classroom through the official curriculum and instruction she delivered, but also in the multitude of ways in which she constructed a safe classroom space and culture. Mrs. Durham led what Antrop-González (2003) has called a "sacrificial life" that is so typical of teachers in sanctuary spaces as she worked to meet her students' survival needs (and often those of their families) and to encourage them to thrive. "For me, my day's never done," she lamented to me. "Whether it's taking something home, grading, or whether it's trying to find a resource for a student, or just worrying about them. I used to say I needed a pen and pencil next to my bed every night to write down things I would randomly think of when I couldn't sleep. [...] Like how can I help?"

Mrs. Durham realized the wide scope of needs of her newcomer students, and she spent long hours completing a multitude of tasks in order to help meet those needs. She explained that although the students were in her classroom to learn English and to earn graduation credits for 9th grade history, the most important things she felt students learned in her classroom were survival skills. She explained, "Obviously learning English, it can be tops, but for me, it's ...[sighs] learning how to survive." She admitted sadly that she felt a lot of her students were not going to be college bound and quickly added that it was not because they were not academically capable, but rather because when it came to needing work to send money home, college became a luxury for which they had neither the time nor financial resources. But "survival skills—just the things that so many kids don't know when they come here—how to manage the system," those were important to teach. She observed, "I mean, it's just [sighs] we have a society of rules and [longer sigh] that, if you're a newcomer to this country, you're not aware of." Her list of things with which students needed her help to "survive" was extensive and daunting.

Mrs. Durham demonstrated care for her students through patience and humor, as well as in the ways she complimented and encouraged students. She provided a physical space that was comfortable and flexible for the students, offering frequent breaks, infusing the space with humor, and planning field trip experiences. Mrs. Durham also provided structure in the classroom, helping the students understand and practice—and sometimes subvert—the rules, but she recognized the individual students' realities and needs within this structure; this often positioned her as a sort of "watchdog" as well.

Mrs. Durham's benevolence in attending to her students' survival needs (i.e., health and safety) meant that she made decisions about what to prioritize in her students' education. She privileged what she perceived her students to need in the immediate term (e.g., housing, food, corrective lenses, dental care) over attending to their long-term aspirations that she felt were out of reach to them (e.g., attending college instead of seeking full-time employment after high school). While it would be easy to accuse Mrs. Durham of "the soft bigotry of low expectations" (Bush, 2000), that accusation is too simplistic and ignores contextual factors. She was contending with the immediacy of young people's lives within institutionalized expectations for them as students. Realistically, for im/migrants who arrive in the United States as adolescents with limited, interrupted, or no formal schooling at all, earning enough academic credits for graduation is often unlikely. Rather than blaming her (or other teachers, for that matter) for prioritizing their immediate needs, it is more productive to examine and interrogate the systematic policies and pressures that force these decisions (i.e., antiquated graduation requirements, English as the language of instruction, etc.). It begs questions about why we, as a society, ask teachers who work with all young people, and specifically with newcomers, to either attend to their students' needs or ignore them. This is an incredibly complex ethical dilemma for Mrs. Durham and others like her.

Mrs. Durham took great care to help students with their basic physical needs (e.g., shelter, transportation), emotional needs (e.g., cultivating friendships and networks of support), and academic needs (e.g., preparing students for upcoming tests and schedule changes). However, she also prepared students for more long-term endeavors, like understanding their rights in the United States—especially in a United States with a President Trump—and helping them learn the symbolic rituals of American citizenship, like standing up to show respect for the flag and more codified demonstrations of citizenship, like voting. In this work in and out of the classroom, Mrs. Sánchez played an important role as well.

MRS. SÁNCHEZ: THE PARAEDUCATOR AND *MAESTRA*

Mrs. Gabriela Sánchez was a Spanish-English bilingual paraeducator who worked at WRHS and was assigned to Mrs. Durham's classroom; her official capacity was that of a translator/interpreter although she was often called upon to tutor and assist students, teachers, and other staff members with a wide range of tasks. She translated a number of communications between the school and students' homes and class materials (e.g., exams and notes outlines), and she interpreted in meetings for enrollment and registration, special education, and attendance concerns. Unofficially, Mrs. Sánchez's position as a paraeducator also positioned her as an assistant to Mrs. Durham, as she helped with or took care of managerial classroom tasks and routines. As is typical of the role of paraeducator, her role was loosely defined and constantly adapted to classroom and school needs and was thus, expansive (e.g., Ernst-Slavit & Wenger, 2006; Hamann, 1995).

Mrs. Sánchez was, in many ways, a mirror of the students with whom she worked. She was in her second year at WRHS, and, at 21 years old, she was just a few years older than most of the students in the classroom. She was a Latinx woman, an immigrant, a recipient of Deferred Action for Childhood Arrivals (DACA), and her first language—like that of most of the students in this classroom—was Spanish; as such, she thought of herself as an English Learner as well. These intersecting identities were important to her role in the classroom and school space and, in important ways, influenced how she sponsored citizenship—especially during a Trump presidency that sought to escalate the criminalization of immigrants and refugees.

She was also a young mother and wife whose two small children and husband were all American-born citizens, and she had taken in a foster daughter who was a student at WRHS, who she treated as a member of her family. Mrs. Sánchez's multiple and intersectional identities modeled for students the construction of a citizen identity mediated by culture. All the various parts of her "being" brought important experiences to bear as she went about her work in this classroom, especially within a political environment emboldened by Donald Trump in which immigrants and people of color are positioned as "less equal" than others and whose rights were deemed negotiable and conditional.

Mrs. Sánchez's first child, her son, was four when I met her. She was almost seventeen years old when she became a mother. Having no support from the child's father in raising her son, she dropped out of high school (not WRHS, but the Catholic high school in Washington River) to care for herself and her young son. She acknowledged that becoming a mother at a young age changed the course of her life. "I mean, there's a lot of things that make me who I am," she explained. "I had to—I chose to drop out because I was embarrassed to come to school while being pregnant." Her mom encouraged her to finish school and she later completed her General Educational Development (GED) diploma. She had also opened her home to a high school-aged foster daughter the previous February, which had come about through her work at the school. It was clear that

26 • LEARNING TO HIDE

Gabriela had grown to love her foster daughter—even through all the frustrations of caring for a teenager—and felt that she was a part of the family. While she acknowledged that her journey had been difficult, she treasured her children.

Mrs. Sánchez had moved to the United States from Mexico with her parents when she was five years old. She did not remember a life in Mexico, but she did value her Mexican heritage. She delighted in showing me photos of her children participating in her church's celebration of the Feast of the Virgin of Guadalupe; her son was dressed in a crisp raw cotton tunic and matching pants with huarache sandals in the style of Juan Diego of Mexican legend, and her daughter wore a matching dress along with a crown of flowers. She held a deep emotional attachment to Mexico, even after having grown up in the United States.

Part of being a Latinx woman was that Mrs. Sánchez lived out the cultural expectations for women, especially wives, to be submissive to their husbands. She expressed frustration about having to ask her husband permission to go out with friends or in what she wore. However, I observed often that she encouraged the young women in the classroom to be strong even under the watchful eyes of the young men in the class. During one such instance, Mrs. Durham, after having given students time to work on a section of the review, asked for "brave volunteers" to share their work on the board. Several girls raised their hands while only one boy raised his, and Mrs. Sánchez observed aloud from her desk, "Las mujeres están dominando el día de hoy *(The women are dominating today.)*." Using the word "mujeres" was a strong message. She didn't call them "girls." Mrs. Durham agreed, saying, "We might not have a woman in the White House, but we have them in the ELL room!" Mrs. Sánchez, having noticed the young women's leadership, used her position in the classroom to affirm that leadership.

Being a Latinx woman also meant that Mrs. Sánchez was racialized as a Person of Color. She, like the students in the classroom, was an immigrant to the United States. As such, she could relate to students' immigrant identities in a way that none of their other teachers could do. Mrs. Sánchez's immigration status was a constant concern for her, as was the case for many of the students. She had applied for and received DACA, and she was hopeful that she would continue on to obtain her residence and then legal citizenship status—which, serendipitously, she gained the very same day that President Trump's executive order rescinded DACA.

Mrs. Sánchez could also relate to students' experiences of being English Learners. Having come to the United States when she was five years old, she had gone to a bilingual kindergarten but remembered her difficulty with English lasting into second grade. She could recall the experience of not understanding and not being understood in English, and she drew on this experience in her interactions with the students. Mrs. Sánchez also understood well how students felt when their language was viewed as a deficiency in learning. She recalled that her kindergarten teacher had been frustrated by her pace in her English language development. She explained, "But so that's why I try to help the kids more and explain things to

The People in the Classroom • 27

them more, so they understand and they don't have that same struggle." She drew on these experiences of learning English—and feeling *deficient*—as she interacted with students in the classroom. Mrs. Sánchez admitted that she still thought of herself as an English learner: "Every day I'm learning more words. There are some words that I don't know what they mean so I just look them up so I know what it means."

Mrs. Sánchez, being a Spanish speaker, was able to communicate with families and parents that many school personnel could not. She was able to do much of the work without having other professionals present; rather than translating or interpreting in these situations, she did the same work as the guidance counselor, nurse, or attendance clerk, but she spoke to the students and families in Spanish instead of English. Thus, Mrs. Sánchez did the same work as many of the professionals in the school but was not compensated in the same way as the professionals in those official positions.

Mrs. Sánchez brought to bear in the classroom multiple intersecting identities and experiences, including being a mother, being a Latinx woman, being an immigrant, and being an English Learner and a Spanish speaker. Mrs. Sánchez was a strong support for the students in this classroom because she could empathize with students. Her immigration and English learning experiences cultivated understanding of what students were going through and helped her equip them with what they would need to move forward. Her liminal DACAmented status allowed her to empathize with the many students who felt that their lives were on hold as they awaited immigration hearings and court dates, and she leveraged her own experiences with an unjust and outdated immigration system to be sure the students were prepared to claim their rights as citizens. She was indeed a support to students, noting that what students needed most was support: "It's support from somebody. Just feel that support. Feel that no matter what you're going through that there's somebody that you can go to all the time."

CONSTRUCTING SANCTUARY IN THE CLASSROOM

The students, Mrs. Durham, and Mrs. Sánchez all played important roles in constructing an environment in which everyone felt valued, safe, and experienced belonging. The students, through shared knowledge of how it felt to be new and to be regarded as different—marked nominally by their label as an English Language Learner—supported each other as they navigated their new lives and constructed new hybrid identities. Mrs. Durham built a physical space full of comfort and safety and a socioemotional space where laughter and levity were welcomed, and Mrs. Sánchez leveraged her intersectional identities to support students and model a citizen identity that proudly integrated her cultural and linguistic identities. In the next chapter, I explore how this space became a sanctuary for students.

CHAPTER 3

CONSTRUCTING SANCTUARY

Classrooms are spaces that both construct and are constructed by the social beings that inhabit them. "Space, as a construct, is both physical and metaphysical; that is, space is both constituted by and constitutes specific sites and also transcends the physical as social actors assign sociocultural interpretations to these sites" (Phillips & Gray, 2021, pp. 10–11). The ELL classroom at Washington River High School was a space that was intentional sanctuary in both physical and figurative ways.

Mrs. Durham's classroom was filled with touches and routines of home, and it was clear that the classroom was designed to offer students spaces to relax as well as to work. Mrs. Durham described her room during an interview: "I've always tried to make this room a family. I've tried to make it more homey *(sic)*, so that it's a safe environment." Even a student new to the classroom in late October, who stood timidly at the front of the classroom with Mrs. Durham and Mrs. Sánchez, within minutes of his arrival and a brief introduction, heard a cheery, "Make yourself at home," delivered with a flourish of her hand around the room. Mrs. Sánchez translated, and the new student scoped out the various spaces to sit and found an empty desk nearby.

The classroom was a space where Mrs. Durham's students—current and former—felt comfortable and safe, and together, the students and adults created a classroom community that reflected the elements of "sanctuary," defined by San-

Learning to Hide: The English Learning Classroom as Sanctuary and Trap
pages 29–44.
Copyright © 2024 by Information Age Publishing
www.infoagepub.com
All rights of reproduction in any form reserved.

dra Bloom (2005) as a "shared experience of creating and maintaining physical, psychological, social and moral safety within a shared environment—any social environment—and thus reducing systemic violence" (p. 16). Mrs. Durham's classroom was a carefully constructed sanctuary in which students and staff experienced comfort, safety, and security balanced with freedom and a sense of belonging fostered through shared moments of playfulness as well as a willingness to be open with one another.

The Physical Classroom Space

It was immediately clear how the classroom space communicated a sense of welcome and comfort. As I crossed through the window-flanked doorway to the hallway in which Mrs. Durham's classroom was located on my first day there, I immediately recognized the familiar scent of the lavender laundry detergent I remembered from my adopted home in Mexico. The scent carried a flood of memories of my time as a college student in Mexico during which I lived with a host family; a second wave of memories rushed over me as I recalled the scent of my own high school Spanish classroom full of Latinx students.

Students lined the walls of the hallway; some sat on the floor with their feet splayed out or crossed in front of them, some stood, and others gathered in small, close huddles. The hall was a flurry of activity but oddly quiet save for the occasional slam of a metal locker. Students spoke in whispers and low voices, and giggles surfaced from one group of girls. Several students looked to be trading homework; I watched one girl shyly approach another who was sitting and quietly speak with her, her head bowed low toward her peer. The girl stood, went to her locker, extracted a piece of lined paper with math equations on it and handed it to the other girl, nodding her acknowledgement of the quiet "gracias" the girl expressed to her and sat back down to rejoin the conversation she had left. The girl who now held the paper sat down and began to copy the answers onto another paper.

Mrs. Durham arrived with her arms loaded with 12-packs of Coke and Sprite along with her personal belongings—two bags hanging from her shoulders. She managed to free one hand as students who crowded around her door reached for the soda packs to help her. Her keys jingled and unlocked the door as she greeted her sleepy-eyed students warmly with smiles and a "good morning" for each of them.

The room was dark as students entered—passing underneath the stars and stripes of the small United States flag hanging low over the doorway—and they all began clicking the switches on each of eight floor lamps placed around the perimeter of the room. Simultaneously, the ceiling illuminated with string lights in the doublewide classroom—having had the middle wall between two classrooms removed a few years prior when the numbers in the English Language Learning program at the high school grew out of their single classroom. The vinyl floor tiles where the wall used to be still showed residual dark marks of the wall's existence.

Constructing Sanctuary • **31**

The rest of the room was comfortable, and clearly divided into different spaces. A stacked set of mailboxes sat atop one shelf along the wall, along with other bookshelves and file cabinets. One cabinet sported an Obama/Biden 2012 bumper sticker and several scattered Pete the Cat stickers. There were two mini-refrigerators on opposite sides of the room—one with a microwave sitting atop it, and the other with a coffee maker and various kitchen utensils beside it.

White boards hung on the walls at each end of the room, and someone had drawn a Mexican flag with a stick figure in the middle on one side. A white board at the front of the room displayed announcements and leftover notes from the previous class session or day. There were also several scattered notes proclaiming, "I love you, Ms. Durham," and reminders for students to leave $1.00 on Mrs. Durham's desk if they took a soda from the refrigerator.

Mrs. Durham's large desk sat diagonally in a corner at the front of the room. Natural light streamed in through the slim floor-to-ceiling window behind her desk. A tall bookshelf and two tables held her computer monitor and keyboard, stacks of papers, books, and the classroom telephone. A furry stuffed Chewbacca toy sat on top of the bookshelf. Mrs. Sánchez's desk was similar to Mrs. Durham's and was located along the far wall in the middle of the room and faced the rows of student desks. Her computer and keyboard shared the desktop with a large desk calendar on which she had marked meeting times in magenta ink. The short bookshelf behind her desk held folded blankets, textbooks, and coffee mugs, and neat stacks of papers and folders.

Posters of all kinds lined the walls of the room: many displayed simple phrases and words in Spanish and English. Students sank into the rows of desks fashioned with the connected chair and writing surface. The back of the room was divided into three smaller spaces by two half-walls—a round table with chairs around it was positioned in the space next to the long window, a higher rectangular table and stools filled the middle space, and a wicker sofa sat in the space leading to the other door of the classroom. Around the perimeter of the rows of desks were a number of other seating options; three students flopped onto the small, worn sofa, almost on top of each other, and shared earbuds connected to one of their cell phones. Framed photographs of students and the teacher and paraeducator sat atop the end tables that flanked the sofa. Other students put their books on their desks, and then rested their heads on top of them. One student—the hood of his sweatshirt pulled up—grabbed a blanket from the shelf behind Mrs. Sánchez's desk, then sat in the rocker, feet up on the ottoman, spread the blankets over his legs, leaned his head back, and closed his eyes. Other groups clustered around desks or the tables at the back of the room. Students laughed and talked, some ate, and others just sat waiting for class to begin.

The school bell sounded in four intermittent muffled beeps, and students in the hallway slammed lockers and scrambled into their classrooms. This, I learned, was the "warning bell," which signaled that class would start in two minutes. A

32 • LEARNING TO HIDE

gradual calm and quiet settled over the room, and students began opening books and arranging notebooks beside them.

The soft lighting, the comfortable seating options, and the accessories like blankets and appliances all created a physical space that was hospitable and homey. Students seemed to feel welcome to make themselves comfortable in a way that is not typical of most high school classrooms: the use of the two classroom microwaves to heat their breakfasts and/or lunches, the readily available purchase of a can of soda for $1.00, the sofas and other seating options, and the personalized mailboxes all made the room a space where they felt comfortable.

One exception to this comfort was that the classroom temperature was normally at 68 degrees Fahrenheit, which Mrs. Durham asserted was too cool for students who were accustomed to tropical climates. She contacted the building's maintenance managers almost daily during the cool and cold weather of late fall and early winter about how she could make her room warmer. The head building maintenance manager dutifully came to measure the heat output and to gauge the temperature in her classroom, but he argued that 68 degrees ought to be warm enough for the room; thus, the blankets provided a temporary solution to the dilemma of the chilly classroom. Finally, in early December, the building maintenance workers succumbed to Mrs. Durham's pleas and installed a thin insulation over her two classroom windows, which did seem to keep the temperature warmer in the room.

Safety and Security

Not only was Mrs. Durham's classroom comfortable, but it was clear that students felt safe in the space as well. Although all students must experience safety and belonging at school, it is especially important to attend to safety in contexts in which students have experienced trauma (Blitz et al., 2016). The discussion of the safety and security fostered in this space could be construed to imply there was something or someone from which or from whom students must be kept safe, or that there was a particular threat to which they were vulnerable. The reality was that many of the students in this classroom had recently had experiences of not being safe, even if it was the feeling of having been not safe. Isabel related clearly the insecurity of what she worried *could* happen in her journey to the United States: "No me sentía segura porque...podían pasar muchas cosas en el camino y no me sentía mucha tranquilidad *(I didn't feel safe because...so many things could happen along the way and I felt uneasy.).*" Saraí and Caterín Michelle, too, described the anxiety they felt along the way and upon arriving in the United States, recalling the uncertainty of the length of their stays in the *perrera*—or even that they were being held in a place called the "dog pound."

When I asked Caterín Michelle if she felt safe at school, she responded with a nod: "Bastante *(Quite)*," and then clarified, "Más que en este salón *(More in this room.).*" Indeed, Mrs. Durham struggled with being absent, knowing that her absence would introduce a stranger into the room and pose potential insecurity for her students. She explained, "[E]ven when I'm not here, having a sub to me, is like, horrible because even when I call in, I'm like, 'OK, here's who you call. And if you can't get one of these three people, then call me back. I'm going in sick.' Because I want somebody that my kids feel safe with."

There were a number of other overt and subtle ways that the room was cultivated as a safe space for everyone in it. The most obvious marker of this safety was the locked classroom door. While class was in session, the door was typically closed and locked. In the mornings, this protocol also served to lock *out* students who arrived at school after the bell signaled the start of school at 7:50 a.m. However, the closed, locked door was also notable in that it was something that all immigrants had been advised to do at home in recent months by civil rights and immigrants' rights organizations like the American Civil Liberties Union (ACLU), the Southern Poverty Law Center (SPLC), and United We Dream (UWD)—especially in light of Donald Trump's promises to deport immigrants in droves. The ACLU's "Know Your Rights" campaign advised immigrants that if the police or Immigration and Customs Enforcement (ICE) came to their home, they should keep the door closed and speak through it to officers. This mirrored the way Mrs. Durham would answer a knock on the door by opening it just a few inches to talk with the through the small gap.

Even when the person or persons who knocked on the classroom door meant no harm, the protocol was an interesting mirror of home. At times, the routine offered a moment of levity as in the instance of a knock at the door, to which a student shouted, "¡No queremos *(We don't want anything!)!*" Several students smirked and looked up to watch the five students from another class who entered and made their way to the back tables to sit down. These students had come in to take a test for another class. The student's response to the knock reminded me of the frequent door-to-door sales visits at my temporary home in Mexico. My host-family mother had explained that I did not have to open the door and greet the salesperson; rather, I should either shout from my second-floor bedroom window or through the front door, "¡No queremos!" While students had not necessarily experienced door-to-door sales in the United States, they clearly knew the protocol for dismissing the unwanted solicitation.

The days following the U.S. general election in November 2016 were perhaps the most noteworthy in how safety was fostered and felt in Mrs. Durham's classroom. On the morning following the announcement of Donald Trump as the 45th President of the United States, the somber mood in the classroom was palpable. Mrs. Durham, after her brief reminder to students that one person cannot make all the decisions, modeled how their lives needed to go on: "Let's try to think of other things today," she said. "I didn't get much sleep last night." Many students went to the hall to get their materials for class, and Mrs. Durham shouted after them to remind them that they needed to switch from history to math. The normalcy of pencils sharpening and lockers slamming was oddly comforting as students began to go about their lives in spite of this new reality full of uncertainty for them. Students got out their math books. They were moving on. It was time for math—Trump or no Trump.

The sense of normalcy she fostered that morning felt, to me, like a form of resistance; students also felt reassured. Caterín Michelle recollected her feelings as she got ready for school that morning, noting, "Sentía como a la vez nerviosa, miedo...sorprendida...me dije, 'wow' *(I felt at the same time nervous, fear... surprised...I was like, 'wow.')*." However, Mrs. Durham's reassurance (and Mrs. Sánchez's hug in the hallway right away in the morning) calmed her; she explained that she felt "mucho más tranquila...por lo que Mrs. Durham nos ha hablado, de lo que nos dijo Mrs. Sánchez...que no solo él toma decisiones *(much calmer...from what Mrs. Durham told us, from what Mrs. Sánchez told us...that he alone does not make decisions)*." She had arrived at school feeling apprehensive and nervous, but her fears were calmed—even if not completely assuaged—with a few reassuring words from Mrs. Durham and a hug from Mrs. Sánchez.

Mrs. Durham was also willing to interrupt class to discuss breaking news and use it to reassure students about their safety at school. On the morning of November 28, 2016, a violent incident occurred on the campus of The Ohio State University; Mrs. Durham switched the projection from her slide presentation to stream a live video following the situation that was unfolding. The students put their pencils down and watched the mayhem on the screen as Mrs. Durham summarized what was happening and Mrs. Sánchez translated. They reported that there had been a shooting—which we later learned was a person wielding a knife—at the university. She briefly explained what was happening and then reminded students, "We've talked about what we would do if we had an active shooter. Run, hide, fight," she recited. She continued, "Washington River does have a plan if something like this were to happen...we have to be quiet if something comes on the speakers...that's how they will notify us." Mrs. Durham considered this news an opportunity to inform students of a tragic event that was unfolding, and also to reiterate to them the protocol should a similar situation happen at their school.

Trauma, understood as prolonged stress that debilitates the body's stress management system, is often attributed to a person's feelings of loss (Blitz et al., 2016). Loss of employment, loss of life or freedom, or loss of home contributes to trauma; immigrants and migrants experience trauma because of the multiple stressors associated with immigration, which could be understood as a loss of home and belonging (Bal & Perzigian, 2013). Given that trauma leads to challenges in the classroom such as distractedness and impulsiveness, safety is a prerequisite for newcomer students' academic achievement (Blitz et al., 2016; Bloom, 2005; Hilburn, 2014).

Freedom

Students enjoyed a freedom not common in most high school classrooms because the room was comfortable, safe, and secure. Notably, their movements were not regulated as rigidly as the norms of high schools usually dictate. Students were able to move between the classroom and their lockers in the hallway with relative freedom, and they often left the classroom during independent work time (i.e., not during instruction) to use the restroom, to get a drink from the water fountain, or to visit the vending machines located in an adjacent hallway in hopes of finding them still operating. Freedom in the classroom maintains a productive learning environment that is cooperative instead of coercive (Shalaby, 2017).

Students enjoyed freedom of movement within the classroom itself as well. For example, one Monday morning, I noted a group of five boys gathering on the couch. Three sat close together on the cushions and two sat on the arms of the sofa. On another day, I entered the classroom to find a tall, lanky male student lying down and covered with a blanket on the floor behind Mrs. Sánchez's desk; he lay directly on the cold tile floor, and his legs extended under Mrs. Sánchez's desk. A girl who appeared to have been sleeping at her desk got up, grabbed another blanket from the shelf, and moved to a chair at the back of the room, spreading the blanket over her legs and arms. Indeed, the seating was normally flexible; I walked in one morning to find six boys congregated around Mrs. Durham's desk, chatting and laughing. One of the boys leaned back comfortably in Mrs. Durham's chair.

Students also had regular opportunities to work together on their assignments or in their preparation for tests. They often congregated in small groups around the room. I remember understanding that I had been accepted as a helping adult after a few days in the classroom when Caterín Michelle, seeing Mrs. Durham and Mrs. Sánchez both occupied helping other students, shyly asked me for help on her assignment. When others saw that I was working with her, three or four of them turned their bodies in our direction; gradually, they and several others slid their desks closer and soon we were working in a small group. After we had worked for a little over a half-hour, Mrs. Durham announced, "¡Tiempo gratis! (Free time!)" and the students scrambled to put their papers and books away.

Students had at least five or ten (and sometimes up to 20) minutes of free time each day, and they took full advantage of it. They ate, drank, chatted with friends, listened to music, and sometimes slept. It was refreshing to see them relax and be so unrestricted. I loved seeing them this way. It reminded me of lazing about in the green space between our classes at my school in Mexico. Students also utilized free time to make up tests or other work they may have missed. Sometimes students worked with Mrs. Durham or Mrs. Sánchez on assignments for other classes they might be taking outside of the English Language Learning program. However, students mostly just used the time to relax and socialize.

Building Trust

This classroom was a comfortable, safe, and secure environment; amidst this comfort, safety, and security, students enjoyed freedoms that not all high school students experience. Another characteristic of this classroom as a sanctuary was the number of ways in which Mrs. Durham, Mrs. Sánchez, and the students fostered a sense of trust in one another to cultivate this classroom climate. Indeed, the range of things that the students and teachers knew about one another required a tremendous amount of trust. The deliberate family atmosphere fostered a strong sense of belonging and commitment to the group; just like a supportive home, students knew the classroom was a space where they could come for help with anything having to do with school or their lives. Relatedly, students knew this classroom was a space where their needs would be met.

Mrs. Durham was deliberate in how she related to her students. She acknowledged that the students with whom she worked needed to believe they could trust her, so she needed to show them they could. She explained, "I've always said so many teachers demand respect in a classroom. I've said from the beginning it's earned in this room, and that goes both ways." She continued, "I can't expect them to have respect for me until they know that I'm gonna respect them and that we have a trusting working relationship, because it's different." The "trusting working relationship" was indeed different from what most teachers found important to establish in their classrooms. She knew that for her to help students with the sensitive issues with which they needed help, she needed to show them they could trust her to keep their confidences, withhold judgment, and be an advocate for them.

The reciprocity of this trusting relationship manifested in how students shared sensitive information about themselves with Mrs. Durham and Mrs. Sánchez that could incriminate them or jeopardize their immigration court cases or jobs. However, for these adults to help them, the students felt that they needed to know details of their situations. It was an enormous risk to trust that these adults would not betray their confidence. For example, many of the students worked in a local meatpacking plant on the overnight cleaning crew—grueling and filthy work. Some students who did this work did not have legal work permits, and they worked under assumed names—names like Doug Smith or Henry Johnson—and Mrs. Durham shook her head at the ethnic mismatch of these names. They provided their employers with identification cards on which the photos looked nothing like them, and they often worked overtime hours without overtime pay. Mrs. Durham and Mrs. Sánchez doubted whether these students were getting paid for the hours they worked, so they had been keeping track of the hours students worked and compared their records to the students' paychecks. Students often stayed past their ending time of 9:30 p.m. until 12:30 a.m. Mrs. Durham had also arranged for students to get school credits for work, so they had to deliver copies of their paychecks to her as documentation. She chuckled as she talked about knowing two names for all her students, their school names and their work names. I wondered how it felt to know something like this about your students, and how the students felt about giving this information to her. They had to believe that she could not or would not report them to authorities for working under false names.

A Place for Help

Mrs. Durham, Mrs. Sánchez, and the students all pitched in to help meet the various needs students brought to the classroom. Their physical needs were met: Students who were hungry received food or were granted the freedom to go to a vending machine to buy a snack; students who were cold could use a blanket to stay warm; and students who needed a drink could go to the drinking fountain or buy a can of soda from Mrs. Durham. However, their emotional needs were met as well. Structure is important in any classroom, and especially important in a classroom like Mrs. Durham's in which so much was happening at once. Mrs. Durham's classroom was a space where students could get help with any number of issues. Students currently or previously labeled "English Language Learners" of all levels came from other general education classes like American Literature or World History to get help or to utilize accommodations while they took a test. Getting help, though, meant cooperating with the rules. Two girls entered the classroom, stage-whispering to Mrs. Durham that they were there to take a test. Mrs. Durham nodded and extended her hand toward them, "Telephones?" They both surrendered their phones to her and walked to the back of the room, taking a seat at opposite sides of the long rectangular table. Later, four more students arrived to take tests. Mrs. Durham assigned them to desks throughout the room, spread apart from one another. They began taking their tests, and a few minutes later, Mrs. Durham hollered, "Biology kids, there's no notes!" in response to seeing a couple of them with notebooks open. Students did not usually argue when Mrs. Durham or Mrs. Sánchez asked them to leave their cell phones on her desk or to put their notes away, although there were times when they put their notes on the floor beside them, face-up, and periodically glanced down at them. Mrs. Durham, however, observed that their notes did not usually provide much help anyway.

Students knew in which subjects Mrs. Durham and Mrs. Sánchez felt comfortable helping them, but it did not stop them from asking for help in the "disliked" subjects. One day, Mrs. Durham sat near a student as she took her test in one of the back desks; she periodically read the questions and multiple-choice responses aloud. Another student approached her with an open computer. Mrs. Durham looked at the computer and exclaimed, "No! I hate American Lit.!" When the student looked at her with a sad but smiling face, she says, "C'mon...let's go sit," and the student followed her to a table at the back of the room. There were always at least a couple of students in the classroom who came from other classes. They worked diligently and accepted help from Mrs. Durham, Mrs. Sánchez, or any of the students who were familiar with the material. Mrs. Durham always had at least two "school-to-career" students whose responsibility it was to assist in the classroom in whatever way they were needed. These students were more proficient in English and often translated or made copies, but often their experiences in courses like American Literature or World History were much more recent than those of the adults in the room. They provided useful help to their peers, sometimes explaining the content in Spanish.

38 • LEARNING TO HIDE

The classroom was a place where students could come when they were hungry. There was usually someone who had food and was willing to share it. Mrs. Durham kept a supply of breakfast food in the classroom and often ate her own breakfast while students were working or enjoying free time. One morning, Mrs. Durham got a pre-packaged Froot Loops bowl out of her desk drawer, went back to the refrigerator for milk, and then grabbed a spoon from Mrs. Sanchez's desk drawer. A student watched her and asked, "¿Tiene uno para mí? *(Do you have one for me?)*" Mrs. Durham, smirking, picked out one morsel and offered it to him. He laughed as he took the green Froot Loop, a big smile on his face. Then Mrs. Durham, adopting a more serious tone, asked, "Did you have breakfast?" He shook his head and she nodded her head toward her desk, taking another bite of her cereal. A minute later, the student opened a drawer in Mrs. Durham's desk and took out an individually packaged bowl of cereal for himself. He walked back to the refrigerator with the bowl of cereal, got milk from the fridge, a spoon from Mrs. Sanchez's desk, and sat down beside Mrs. Durham to eat it. Although Mrs. Durham teased the student about sharing only a tiny morsel of the food with him, she inquired about whether he had eaten breakfast and then gave him the okay to take something to eat from her desk.

Students were met in the days following the U.S. general election in November 2016 with countless rumors and suppositions about the security of their futures in the United States. Fear and anxiety lurked just below the surface due to the possibility of Trump's campaign promises, and understandably, these emotions interfered with class work and focus. On the Friday morning following the election, Mrs. Durham wondered aloud to me about what she could do to help her students. When the bell sounded to signal the start of class, she hastily greeted her students and then asked them to rearrange their desks into one large circle while she searched for sheets of large white paper. It appeared that she was changing her lesson plan on the fly. When the students were all seated, she told them that she had heard so many questions and rumors about what Trump's election would mean for the students and their families and friends. She instructed them to get into groups of about four students and, using Google Translate on their phones, take about 20 minutes to write down any questions or concerns they had. "Together we'll go through and figure out the answers," she assured them. After about 20 minutes had passed, Mrs. Durham collected their papers and students returned to sit in the large circle; each paper had between five and ten questions or comments written.

Mrs. Durham sighed as she read the first question: "Can [Donald Trump] take away what has already been given?" This question referred to settled or pending immigration cases. She leaned back, answering slowly, the tapping of her fingertips on the desk in front of her punctuating her response. "If you were born here, you are a citizen. There's no changing that." When Mrs. Sánchez translated the response, the words hung heavily over the room; it was clear that the gaping silence about those *not* born in the United States did not assuage their fears about their own fates or those of their family members. Mrs. Durham continued down their lists of questions and concerns with Mrs. Sánchez translating to Spanish. Their questions revealed their confusion and anxieties: "Is [Donald Trump] going to deport us? Will [he] remove work permits from Hispanics? Why doesn't [Trump] like Hispanics? What will happen with people who have immigration process in court? Is it true that there will be racism? Is it true that he erected the wall and removed the papers from the people?" Clearly, students were preoccupied with how the vote would impact their lives.

Many of the questions did not have easy or even *any* answers, but Mrs. Durham sensed they needed to voice their thoughts. Caterín Michelle acknowledged that the open airing of their concerns and questions made her feel calmer—not oblivious to reality, but calmer. This impromptu discussion was a direct response to a need Mrs. Durham perceived in her students, and they understood more about the situation after their discussion. This comforted students and carved space for them to get answers and voice concerns about their immediate lives.

Levity and Playfulness

Within a loaded sociopolitical environment, there were also moments that fostered levity and playfulness in the classroom, often memorialized with photographs. Mrs. Durham and Mrs. Sánchez took opportunities to dress up in costume, and students giggled and feigned eye rolls at their get-ups. On Halloween, I rounded the corner to the classroom and through the glass partition I saw Mrs. Durham standing in the middle of the hall dressed as a zombie prom queen. Her hair was sprayed stiff to within an inch of its life, and the spray gave her hair a grayish color. A jeweled crown sat atop her head. She wore a ripped-up pink prom dress, gray smudges across the tulle ruffles. Her bare arms, shoulders, and face were brushed with a gray powder, making her appear pale and eerily "undead."

Mrs. Sánchez was dressed like the Disney princess, Jasmine, with long flowing pants that tightened at the ankle and gold bangles hanging from the edges of her shirt. She wore a loose sweater over the top, given that "it took forever" to find something at the store that her husband would let her wear; most of the things she tried were too low-cut or too tight, she said. None of the students were dressed in costume. Students all took turns snapping photos with Mrs. Sánchez and Mrs. Durham, adding in people to get group photos as well. Clearly, photos were an important way to document their time together. I could not help but be drawn in by the giggles and hilarious poses the costumes elicited. Although none of the students dressed up in costume on that day, they took other opportunities to dress up for bonus points; several of the students wore red, white, and blue to commemorate Veterans Day, and of course, their outfits were documented with photos.

Another example of an inside joke in the classroom was *la chancla*, which means *sandal* in Spanish. Waving a shoe or even just pretending to wave a shoe was a ritual threat when someone misbehaved or tried to bother another. For example, when one student playfully attempted to steal another classmate's breakfast, he was met with the threat of *la chancla*. Mrs. Durham yelled teasingly, "*La*

40 • LEARNING TO HIDE

chancla!" I look at her questioningly, and she asked me, "You don't know *la chancla*?" I shook my head and she insisted, "You have to Google *chancla* videos." Sure enough, I did. As soon as I saw the first one—a woman using her sandal to fight off a crocodile from attacking her dog—I realized that of course I knew *la chancla*! The students laughed about how their moms teasingly threatened their children with their *chanclas* by taking one off and shaking it at them or chasing them around with it.

Another inside joke mentioned earlier began with Mrs. Durham's attempt to reassure students that they would be safe in the United States after the election of Donald Trump. When she jokingly reassured them that they had a safe place to stay in her basement, the joke lived on for weeks. Even with the prospect of a safe space in Mrs. Durham's basement, students stayed realistic about the possibility of their having to leave the United States. Days after the election, a student entered the room before the bell, imploring Mrs. Durham to take it easy on them. "Don't give us a lot of work; we don't have a lot of time left," he said. Several students laughed, and another student asked if they could have a party in her basement "before [they had to go] back to El Salvador." Mrs. Durham, in mock seriousness, replied, "Well, it's a small basement, but it's a basement!" Students listening to the exchange exclaimed, "Woo!" and exchanged high-fives, and laughter erupted all around.

These inside jokes became rituals as students and their teachers used them to prompt a predictable response of laughter and smiles. These kinds of rituals provided moments of much-needed levity as they grappled with the vitriol and uncertainty of the sociopolitical context.

Belonging

Students experienced belonging in this space and felt that their full histories were valued here. The sense of belonging is an important element in constructing sanctuary (Antrop-González, 2003; Bloom, 2005). Mrs. Durham described the community in her classroom powerfully when I asked her what she thought was the most important thing students learned in her classroom: "Most important thing about this classroom is that it's a family. Like having that sense of belonging. […] I guess I've also told the kids, 'You know you have your family you're born with and then you have your family that you create—not necessarily through marriage—but you have your own family,' and that's what this room is." Indeed, a sense of family helps to create an inclusive space, which is one of the dimensions of schools—and in this case, classrooms—as sanctuaries. Attending to the cultivation of a familial classroom community fosters a sense of belonging and healthy relationships (Antrop-González, 2003).

Looking around the room it was clear that the classroom reflected the stories of those who inhabited it and affirmed students' biographies. The multitude of photographs clustered on laminated poster boards documenting the lived experiences of students and adults in the classroom were reminiscent of the kinds of photographs hanging on the walls of my own family's home. Photo albums were piled high in one of the cabinets, and students often looked through them, marveling at how Mrs. Durham had changed and asking about people they may have recognized.

A cluster of maps hung on one wall of the classroom. There was a map of every home country of the students in the classroom. Students had written their names on adhesive arrows and placed them with the tip of the arrow pointing to their hometown. Alejandro's name stood alone on the map of Costa Rica. A handful of students, including Isabel, had placed their names on the map of El Salvador. Only five names were on the map of Mexico; one of them was Mrs. Sánchez, whose name pointed to the area of Durango in the north central region of Mexico. Three students' names pointed to cities in the northwestern area of Honduras. The map of Guatemala was a collection of arrows going this way and that. Thirty-seven names were on the map of Guatemala, with a large cluster around the capital of Guatemala City. These maps visually displayed the various places from which they had all come to share this space.

Sitting atop the counter-height shelves in the back of the classroom rested three tiny, embroidered blouses. The blouses, sewn from raw cotton and embroidered in Oaxacan style—with reds, greens, yellows, and blues threaded into intricate designs—were crafted by three students for an art project, and they wished to leave them for decoration in Mrs. Durham's classroom. The integration of the students' artwork was another way that made the space theirs.

Caterín Michelle recalled her first days in the classroom during which she sensed the trusting and supportive environment, seeing that her classmates spoke openly with each other and the teachers. She did, however, admit that it was daunting to imagine herself fitting into this tightly knit community. Anyelín likewise observed that new students, as she had once been, might be overwhelmed by the constant activity that happens in the room, but she added that it was the responsibility of those already there to help them feel welcome. This demonstrated her feeling that the members of the classroom all belonged, and that they all worked together to make it a community.

The ELL classroom at Washington River High School was a sanctuary for the newcomer students (and their teachers) who entered it. The comfortable, safe environment was a space where students felt secure in the knowledge that their needs would be met. They had freedom to move around and talk to one another, which made the room a very human space. Playfulness was a norm that made the space at once enjoyable and provided levity in otherwise dark moments. The shared building of this community fostered trust and mutual respect. This classroom was a space in which there was a mutual trust between the students and adults. They built respect by being open with one another and by taking care of each other's needs, including emotional, physiological, and psychological needs, which made the classroom a typically cheerful and supportive space in which students and adults felt valued.

SANCTUARY TO WHAT END?

This classroom was a sanctuary for the students and adults in it, and all the members of the classroom co-constructed it. From the touches of home—like blankets and soft lighting—to the sharing of food and their life stories, the adults and students alike created a space in which everyone felt they belonged. The physical safety and emotional security students experienced in this classroom fostered an environment built around trusting relationships and respect for the group.

Sanctuary from What?

The very definition of a sanctuary—understood as a physically, psychologically, socially, and morally safe space (Bloom, 2005)—implies that there is something from what or someone from whom the students and adults in this classroom ought to be kept safe. Indeed, the students in the classroom felt safe there—but safe from what?

Caterín Michelle discussed in great detail how scary and stressful her journey from Honduras to the United States had been for her and her siblings. The journey through the poverty-stricken country of Guatemala and the dangers presented by the Mexican highways were difficult, but she came from Honduras, the country with the world's highest per capita homicide rate and other instances of gang-related violence (Pew Research Center, 2014b; United States Department of State, 2017). She felt safe to even walk outside to go to school when she arrived in Washington River, and as she mentioned, she felt the safest in Mrs. Durham's classroom. Other students felt the same, and similarly had come from places where their physical safety was not a certainty each day. Given the sparse access to blankets and mattresses in the *perreras* and refugee homes, students found the conditions of this classroom to be comfortable and safe.

Students also needed emotional sanctuary from the relentless barrage of reminders that they were outsiders in the United States. Immigration in a Trump administration was an experience fraught with racist alienation and nativist claims to the superiority of the rights of U.S.-born citizens. The Trump administration's calls for strict enforcement of immigration laws that purported to rid the country of "bad hombres" instilled in refugees and undocumented immigrants a fear of deportation, detention, and separation from their families. Trump's rhetoric effectively constructed a relationship between crime and immigrants, and immigrant arrests increased under his orders, although actual deportations decreased (Bendix, 2017). Even recipients of the Deferred Action for Childhood Arrivals (DACA) status felt threatened under the new administration, especially after having given up their personal information to the government in their application for DACA. Schools were spaces that immigration enforcement officers were encouraged to avoid, and students felt uncertain that this would continue to be the case. In this classroom students were allowed to ask questions about their rights, and the adults actively took steps to inform students of them.

Newcomers also needed cognitive respite from the relentless barrage of English as they develop their language skills—especially since it was clear to them that learning English ought to be their first goal. My own experience of immersion in a second language was exhausting, humbling, and stressful. I recall feeling at once ignorant and vulnerable even as I gained proficiency; I told my friends back in the United States that I felt as if I could not express myself or allow my true self to be known without a common language to do so. I could not be funny or even understand others' jokes, and I could not even communicate confidently to buy what I needed in a store. These students' experiences in Washington River resonated with memories of my experience, but I was keenly aware that my experience had been a choice. These students—at a much younger age than I had been—faced their new realities in a country that privileges English. This classroom served as a space where students could leverage their full linguistic repertoire and in which their language(s) served as a resource for themselves and each other.

Sanctuary for *What?*

Conceptualizing the classroom as a sanctuary also implies that there are reasons that it ought to be a sanctuary for newcomer students. I offer three justice-oriented reasons the sanctuary classroom for newcomers supports the development of democratic citizens: 1) the development of their "hybrid" identities; 2) learning their rights and responsibilities as citizens of and in the U.S.; and 3) to have the opportunity to choose their life paths.

Students who arrive in the U.S. as children and adolescents need a safe "in-between space" (Sarroub, 2002) in which they can negotiate their "hybrid" identities, fusing and integrating their various cultures to construct new identities (Irizarry, 2007). This classroom was a space in which all aspects of students' lives were affirmed and valued, and they were encouraged to acknowledge their full biographies as they transitioned into a life in the United States.

Students, especially because they are positioned as "people of color" in the United States, also have a unique need to learn their rights and responsibilities as citizens in a raced, classed society to claim space and belonging in the full public realm (Ladson-Billings, 2004), and it is most appropriate for them to do so in a safe space. It was even more important in the political climate of the Trump administration for students to learn how they could resist the restrictions on their rights, and this remains true into the fourth year of the Biden administration.[1]

Finally, these students' experiences of high school were notably different from their English-proficient counterparts in general education classes. These students were tasked with learning English at the same time as they were completing cred-

---

[1] Despite his ambitious promises to undo many of the Trump administration's immigration policies that criminalized and dehumanized immigrants and migrants (i.e., detaining people at the border and/or forcing people entering through the U.S.'s southern border to seek asylum to wait in Mexico for their cases to be considered), President Biden's administration has struggled to advance any influential changes in immigration policy.

its for graduation. If they are to have access to choose their life paths—whether that includes college or not—they need a space that looks and feels safe and affirming. That is, they need a space where they learn and are free to amplify their voices, claim their rights, and to heal and grow from any traumatic experiences and leverage their full life histories in their education. A healthy, vital, and socially just democracy requires it.

CHAPTER 4

MISMATCH

The ELL classroom at Washington River High School was most certainly a sanctuary for students—sanctuary *from* the outside world that rendered them "different" and even dangerous, and sanctuary *for* negotiation of their identities and affirmation of belonging. However, the sanctuary of the classroom also allowed for newcomer students to remain hidden from the rest of the school community and for the wider school community to remain essentially unphased by their presence. The life of this classroom and school constructed and revealed a stark duality—the "mismatch" of students' realities and the school's extant policies. Deschenes et al. (2001) note:

> There have always been students who do not meet the educational expectations of their time—students outside the mainstream mold who do not fit dominant notions of success. The differences between schools and these students can be thought of as a "mismatch" between the structure of schools and the social, cultural, or economic backgrounds of students identified as problems. (p. 525)

Even though Mrs. Durham's classroom provided sanctuary for her students, due to the mismatch between them and the school, this sanctuary had boundaries and confined them to a limited space for the development of citizen identities.

The students in this classroom lived dual lives in many ways. Some were by age adolescents, but by life experience adults. Some worked full-time jobs and

---

Learning to Hide: The English Learning Classroom as Sanctuary and Trap
pages 45–53.
Copyright © 2024 by Information Age Publishing
www.infoagepub.com
All rights of reproduction in any form reserved.

46 • LEARNING TO HIDE

attended school full-time, and all of them had dreams tempered with a realist perspective about what was plausible for their futures. The dual lives of these students asked them to imagine more realistic dreams for themselves, and to understand how the context in which they lived in the United States limited the possibilities of what they could pursue as dreams. Their marginality at school perpetuated a marginal existence in the larger community.

THE MISMATCH OF SCHOOL
RULES AND STUDENTS' REALITIES

The newcomer students in WRHS experienced duality in their everyday realities. They were at once adolescents and adults, being teenagers starting at a new school and dealing with the stress of acculturation that bespoke their very adult lives—getting the required immunizations, consulting with immigration attorneys, and securing housing and jobs. Students who held jobs faced the duality of being a worker and a student—many of them working under an assumed name that literally marked this duality. Students negotiated the duality of being a human—"equal in dignity and rights" (United Nations, 1948)—and of being an immigrant in the United States—a criminalized identity that racialized them and qualified their rights based on legal status (Catalano, 2017; Santa Ana, 2002). Students also lived the duality of dreaming of a future they would choose for themselves and the need to be realistic about the financial and legal limitations of those dreams. Finally, the newcomer students' native language(s) were necessary and meaningful at home and often at work but were marginalized and pathologized at school as they became "English Learners," framing a duality between linguistic and cultural *proficiency* and *deficiency*.

The extant policies, expectations, and operational procedures of school simultaneously constructed these dual realities while not acknowledging, accommodating, or leveraging them for learning. Students navigated school by breaking rules and mapping the margins of school to work around the mismatches. The school managed newcomers as a problem, and the structure of their classes communicated to them that learning English was their most important goal in school.

The Duality of Students' Lives

Many students in the classroom left school to go to work. Some of them—those who were able to get an identification card that listed an older age or in some cases the name of an authorized worker—worked at a local meatpacking plant on the overnight cleaning crew. Others worked shifts at McDonald's, and some worked at a semi-truck trailer washout service. Students sometimes were able to earn elective credits for work experience, and they submitted their timesheets to Mrs. Durham to document their hours. Those who worked under names that were not their given names masked those names and wrote their given names.

Jorge, a tall and lumbering kid, walked in one Monday morning and said sleepily to Mrs. Durham, "I trabajo *(work)* all weekend." Mrs. Durham replied sympathetically, "O mi gatos. O-eme-ge *(both expressions like 'Oh my gosh' and 'OMG')*." She had a brief conversation with him about getting enough sleep and not working too much. Anyelín, who worked five to six hours each night, insisted that it was "easy work" and that five or six hours each night was "not a lot." Working hours like those did not leave much time for adequate sleep or for participation in extracurricular school activities or time to relax at home.

Sometimes students had to choose between being a student or a worker, given attendance requirements. Mrs. Sánchez described one student who quit school because he was offered a morning position at the meatpacking plant. He was 18 years old, and an opportunity to work daytime hours instead of overnight was more lucrative to him than staying in school with limited prospects to graduate before he aged out of the system. Mrs. Sánchez shook her head and said, "Everyday stories..." her voice trailing off. Her husband worked at the same plant as she had as well, and she understood well how infrequently the coveted daytime positions at the plant became available.

Posters hanging in the hallways around the school invited students to dream about what they wanted for their futures. The opportunity to attend college figured prominently in these messages and communicated that big dreams required a college degree. Even in Mrs. Durham's classroom, college pennants hung from the tops of the walls. College, though, was not a realistic option for many of the students in Mrs. Durham's classroom.

All the students, except one, in the classroom were immigrants, and some were either seeking refugee status or were caught up in a backlogged immigration court. While United States history textbooks often romanticize immigration as an inspirational, aspirational, hopeful experience, the students in Mrs. Durham's classroom recognized their own experiences when they learned about Dred Scott, who lived when "a slave was *not a citizen* and *had no rights*" because the "Constitution protected slavery" (Duran et al., 2005). Being "not a citizen" and "having no rights" resonated with many of the students in the classroom, and those words felt heavy as the students copied them into their notes. While many of them told of their dreams to become a graphic designer (Sayra) or just to have a good job to be able to take care of their parents (Saraí, Jesús, Caterín Michelle, and many others), they also acknowledged the reality that college was expensive and that they were in more immediate need of financial resources.

The anti-immigrant rhetoric and the promise of mass deportations of the Trump presidential campaign and eventual victory no doubt influenced how these students imagined their futures. In the days following the general election, when the students had an opportunity to write concerns and questions they had about what Trump's election would mean for them, they worried about deportation—whether they had immigration papers or not—and how Trump's policies would affect their opportunities to work. One group asked, "Will remove *(sic)* work permits from

48 • LEARNING TO HIDE

hispanics *(sic)*?" They referenced "hispanics" here, and not all immigrants; to them, the anti-immigrant rhetoric was aimed at them.

Some students worried that they might lose the right to sponsor a family member after being granted legal status, and some were concerned about what would happen to undocumented parents of American citizens. Others worried more generally about the ways Trump could institutionalize discrimination based on sexual orientation and gender identity. They also felt as if Trump's rhetoric had opened the door to more overt everyday racism and discrimination, asserting, "People judge by how I loock *(sic)*." They described feelings of fear, anger, sadness, surprise, and betrayal, wondering why some "Hispanics" voted for Trump.

The students acknowledged the way they were positioned in the context of a Trump administration, and dreams seemed to be a luxury they could not afford. Caterín Michelle admitted that she had thought about college and even talked with her mom about it, but her mom had told her that college "is so expensive." She tilted her head and explained that "ever since [she] was little, [her] dad always told [her] that [she] would be a doctor someday." Now, though, what she wanted for her future was a "good-paying job," one in which she would get along well with her boss.

Jesús, while asserting that his future was "en las manos de Dios *(in God's hands),*" could see himself working in an office, maybe a bank, or even in a grocery store. College, he said, would be difficult because of "recursos económicos *(financial resources)*." Saraí said that what she wanted was a "good future" in which she could help her mother because she had helped Saraí and her sister so much, and she wanted to be able to give that back to her. Had Saraí remained in Guatemala, she would have been starting her career training as a nurse; here in the United States, she did not know how she could go about pursuing a career in nursing.

Breaking the Rules and Hiding from Surveillance

One further duality of most of the students in this classroom was that of being a student and an adult. Students at WRHS had to contend with rules that limited what they could do at school and, therefore, limited how they could function in their adult roles. Students learned either to hide or to overtly break the rules to do what they needed to do (e.g., take phone calls under a "no cell phone" policy). They also constructed a network of safe spaces in which they sought help, moving quickly from place to place until they got ahead of the policing of their behavior. For Mateo, the "no cell phone" policy meant that if he wanted to help his father with his immigration case by speaking with his immigration attorney, he needed to frantically gain permission to break the rule or suffer the consequence of having his phone confiscated and withheld from him for the rest of the day.

> Mateo's phone buzzed and he looked at Mrs. Sánchez pleadingly as he held up his phone to her. He walked to the back of the room to answer the call without

having gotten her permission. Mrs. Durham, noticing him, yelled, "What the heck, Mateo?!?" Mrs. Sánchez was quick to calm her, "It's his father." This was a game-changer; Mrs. Durham nodded and walked back to the front. Mateo's father's attorney had called him—in school—to discuss his father's immigration case. Mateo had handled two 'adult' situations—the attorney phone call and facilitating introductions between a new student who shared his native Mam language and Mrs. Durham and Mrs. Sánchez—in the last hour. He was at once a youth and an adult.

Mateo's cell phone use—even though it was not during instruction—was policed, and he was forced to break the rule or risk missing the opportunity to speak with his father's attorney. The "no cell phone" policy and other rules of school were clearly not sensitive to the students who handled adult situations like Mateo did.

Students were also policed as they searched for help. EL students who were enrolled in a general education class often came to Mrs. Durham's classroom for assistance on their assignments and exams for these classes. Since their general education classes (i.e., art, American Literature, physical education, etc.) were conducted in English, they often sought help in understanding the content. One student demonstrated how students searched for help and when they were denied help, went to the next stop in their network of safe spaces. They were policed, however, as they scurried from one stop to the next.

> A student came into the classroom to take a final exam and Mrs. Durham told him that she needed to find out what she would be able to do to help. She left to go talk with the teacher, and the student rolled his eyes dramatically in frustration. A few minutes later, Mrs. Durham returned and said to him, "I can't read 'cold reads' but I can read and translate questions." The student's shoulders fell, and then he asked, "Can I go to the PAC room?" *This is a room where all students can get assistance with any of their classes.* Mrs. Durham shot back sharply, "They aren't going to help you any more than I am," and she turned away. She mumbled, intimating what she thought the student was thinking, "Let me go somewhere else to see if I can manipulate..." and her voice trailed off. *It must get to her to have to police this kind of thing.*

> The student left and Mrs. Sánchez went to the PAC room to tell the paraeducators there about the limitations of the help he could receive on the work he had. She returned a few minutes later and reported to Mrs. Durham that the student had already been getting help from the bilingual paraeducator in the PAC room. They rolled their eyes in mutual frustration.

In this case, the student was able to get to the PAC room before Mrs. Sánchez arrived to tell the paraeducators there the limitations of the help he could receive. This routine of policing seemed more focused on catching students in the act of "manipulating" the system than on critiquing the system that they felt the need to manipulate.

Rules certainly have a place in school, but it would be wise to reconsider the rules in light of newcomer students' realities. How are newcomers involved in constructing the rules by which they live, an important practice of the democratic

50 • LEARNING TO HIDE

citizen? In this case, the imposed rules of school did not include space for students to participate in the deliberation of making of them; instead, through the hegemonic status quo a central practice of their citizenship became learning to hide and to subvert these mismatched mandates.

Learning English Was More Important than Learning Course Content

Students learned through the policies and practices at school that learning English was more important than mastering the content of their core classes (see, for example, Abedi, 2004). This was especially problematic in the case of social studies, a program of study explicitly aimed at developing democratic citizens. Privileging English also meant that students equated knowing English with being smart.

Caterín Michelle noted that she relied on Alejandro for help with history because he "es el más inteligente porque sabe más inglés *(is the smartest because he knows more English)*." Alejandro's proficiency in English afforded him faster, easier access to the content because the content was delivered in English. Even with Mrs. Sánchez's translations in Spanish, the students had only the one opportunity to understand the content in Spanish. If they were to reread the text, their notes, or the study guide as review for an exam, it was all in English. This sent a clear message that students needed to understand English before they could understand the content; English was positioned as a prerequisite to learning U.S. history. Anyelín acknowledged as much when she explained in frustration that she did not remember anything from history class because she needed to learn more English first.

Mrs. Durham's sheltered U.S. history class provided an illustration of how newcomer students were able to earn graduation credits while they were learning English. This structure was an attempt to beat the clock that most newcomer students faced because they arrived with few credits that could be applied toward graduation and had many to earn before they reached 21 years of age (i.e., when the state was no longer required to provide free public education). However, it also revealed the haste and shallowness with which the material in the class was covered in attempts to make it accessible to newcomers in English.

The class offered important observations about what is actually learned and not learned in these kinds of classes. Mrs. Durham's history class was conducted in English—with one-time translations in Spanish—and as such, English was positioned as more important than the history content. Furthermore, the textbook, ironically titled, *Access American History* (Duran et al., 2005), was in English only and included content that was taught in middle school-level general education history classes in the district (even though the content was aligned to 9th grade standards at WRHS). Students took scripted notes in English and copied those same notes on the routine worksheet; the absence of discussions about the course content contributed to a shallow and monolithic understanding—at best—of U.S.

history and how it has shaped our present. Further, it neglected to acknowledge how the students in the room were positioned within the past, present, and future United States.

Newcomer students need to learn American history (including the evolution of the rights and responsibilities of citizenship) if they are to develop a fuller understanding of their positionality and agency in U.S. society. They also need to learn English if they are to navigate the institutional structures that constitute the American democracy, even though English is not the official language of the United States. However, in the case of Mrs. Durham's classroom in which students were engaged with learning U.S. history through English, the experience was counterproductive; students neither felt comfortable with the content nor with their English language development as a result. They looked to Alejandro, whose English was more developed, as the only student knowledgeable about U.S. history. This was problematic, obviously, and supports the idea of a U.S. history class taught in Spanish. The persistence of English as the language of instruction demonstrated the school's perpetuation of an ideology that privileges English and an unwillingness to draw on the students' "funds of knowledge" to help them learn (Gonzalez et al., 2005; Moll et al., 1992).

What did this teach newcomers vis-à-vis their positionality and roles as citizens? Ultimately, they learned that their linguistic repertoires were not valued in the United States and that acquisition of English was the rite of passage that would earn them the right to be seen and heard in United States discourse and public space. Moreover, students learned a history that was a stripped down, majoritarian version of American history that dismissed the nuances of multiple perspectives. Critical thinking was noticeably absent, which constructed a citizenship practice of unquestioning compliance.

Newcomers Were a Problem for the School

Stemming from the mismatches between the Spanish-speaking newcomers from Mexico and Central America to this Midwestern community of mostly white monolingual English-speaking residents, the newcomers were viewed as a problem by the school. This was evident in how the newcomer students were segregated, marginalized, and ignored within the school. Their placement in the ELL program meant that they had all but one class in the ELL hallway and rarely ventured outside of it. The school made few—if any—attempts to acknowledge and integrate the newcomer students' cultures and experiences into the school, and perhaps more problematically, I'm not sure they even acknowledged how they *could* or *should* have integrated newcomers into the school community.

The morning announcements were a daily reminder that the school did not acknowledge the presence of its newcomers, or if they did, that the announcements in English would not be accessible to them. The announcements droned on and on, usually for almost five minutes, all in English. Given the ways in which the school leveraged the bilingualism of some students to translate (for free) in

52 • LEARNING TO HIDE

classes, it was surprising to me that announcements were never offered in Spanish. Since they announced the offering of ACT test prep classes, reminders to display parking passes, and odds and ends about team practices and meetings, I wondered how the students who were not English-dominant got their school-wide announcements. Did Mrs. Durham and Mrs. Sánchez act as the intermediary for the news they received about school events and other announcements? The message was clear that the announcements did not apply to an audience who did not speak English; the school did not see it as a priority to be certain that *all* students had firsthand access to the announcements. Mrs. Durham admitted, "They miss *so much* of that stuff because it's not in their language. Same thing with pep rallies or an assembly. There just needs to be more done in both languages. And I don't know how you necessarily do that without... [sigh] I mean, it's time-consuming."

Some actors in the school actively shirked their responsibility to serve the needs of Spanish-speaking students and their families. The attendance clerk (and the administrators who supervised her) who stopped making calls to families to verify student absences clearly did not think it was her (their) responsibility to find a way to communicate with these families. The nurse's office and guidance office demonstrated the same kind of response to newcomers. The students' and families' Spanish dominance was viewed as a problem; thus, the monolingual English speakers working in these offices bore no responsibility in adapting to meet the realities of the newcomers, and Mrs. Durham and Mrs. Sánchez took on their responsibilities as well.

Isabel's experience of Spanish class—an introductory-level Spanish class—demonstrated how her proficiency in Spanish was ignored. In this class, she told me, she did "the same thing as the white kids—repeat everything." I was frustrated by the unavailability of the course for proficient Spanish speakers that I had designed and taught at WRHS less than seven years earlier, and I wondered how many students sat in an introductory Spanish class that privileged Castilian Spanish over Central American and Mexican dialects. At the same time that the school ignored Isabel's Spanish *pro*ficiency, the school labeled her and others like her as *de*ficient in English; this deficiency was viewed as a problem to be remedied with her isolation in the ELL program.

How did this positioning of newcomer students as a problem influence their construction of citizen identities? Students understood well that they were entering an institution that was not designed by or for them. Again, their citizenship practices were aimed at compliance with a system that identified only their perceived deficits and drew upon their proficiencies only when it served the purposes of the school (i.e., as translators and interpreters), what Derrick Bell (2009) calls "interest convergence." Newcomer students, then, experienced exclusion in the school, even as they experienced belonging in the ELL classroom, and this exclusion conveyed messages about the limited scope of their membership in the larger community.

EVADING TRANSFORMATION

Washington River High School and its newcomer students were a mismatch within the longstanding structure of school in Washington River; that is, their cultural, linguistic, and socioeconomic backgrounds were regarded as problems. In terms of linguistic mismatch, the "business" of the school was conducted in English—and with interpreters in Spanish—and prompted an urgency for new students to learn English, but there was not a reciprocal urgency for teachers or other school professionals to learn Spanish or to hire multilingual teachers. Students' already-established proficiency in Spanish was not necessarily helpful in Spanish classes either; learning English was privileged over developing their Spanish language skills, and their Spanish was deemed second-class in relation to the Castilian Spanish taught in Spanish classes (see, for example, Leeman, 2018). This is a longstanding debate in the education of newcomer students—whether to cultivate and draw upon bilingualism or to immerse them in English (Valdés, 2001); few would argue that English is not important in the education of newcomers, but privileging English neglects the possibilities of "bilingual literacies" and "translanguaging" in learning (Fránquiz & Salinas, 2011; García & Wei, 2014).

Next, the students' dual lives required that they break rules or hide to fulfill their obligations as family members and friends, and the policing of students' behaviors in school mirrored that of the criminalization of immigrants in governmental policies like California's Proposition 187 and the Immigration Reform and Control Act of 1986. This criminalization cultivated citizenship practices aimed at hiding, including compliance with a system mismatched to their realities and silence in their resistance to this system.

Finally, WRHS problematized and segregated newcomer students, which expands Hamann's (2003) descriptions of NLD community responses to newcomers—xenophobia, disquiet, and welcome—to include *evasion*. Washington River's response demonstrates evasion because the school, having segregated newcomer students in a single hallway of the school for the majority of the school day, did not purposefully invite or integrate them into the larger school context in any meaningful way. This segregation provides an apt illustration of Valdés's (2001) description of the "ESL ghetto"; however, it also speaks to Sarroub's (2002) concern for a safe "in-between space" in which newcomers can negotiate their "hybrid" identities.

The students in the ELL classroom at WRHS clearly felt belonging inside the classroom, but they did not experience this belonging in other places in the school. This marginalization limited their experience of the public realm within the school and relegated them to the periphery of the life of the school. The multidimensional mismatches between the school and their newcomer students—and the school's evasion of the transformation the mismatches could prompt—conveyed that the school was not for them, and that assimilation was the goal.

CHAPTER 5

THE IMPLICATIONS OF CARE

The caring relation in teaching is undergirded by a desire to foster growth in others and to connect in meaningful relationships (Noddings, 1988; Valenzuela, 1999). Schools, as stratified and competitive institutions, privilege achievement grounded in English dominance and cultural scripts of meritocracy (Labaree, 2010). As such, they often overlook or willfully ignore the importance of relational learning experiences for students.

The students in this classroom described their teachers[1] as "helpful" and "caring"—qualities they attributed to "good people." Likewise, the students sought help, support, and camaraderie from each other; they befriended one another easily in this space, having so much in common and spending most of their school day together. Mrs. Durham and Mrs. Sánchez both mentioned on several occasions how much they cared about their students; however, their words and actions expressed care very differently. The ways in which different people demonstrated care in the classroom conveyed important implications for the purposes of schooling for newcomer students and for their development as citizens.

The aims of schooling, whether explicit or implicit, shape the life and work inside of them. Labaree (1997), for example, offers three conflicting aims of

---

[1] I use the term "teachers" to include Mrs. Durham and Mrs. Sánchez because the students referred to both of them as teachers.

Learning to Hide: The English Learning Classroom as Sanctuary and Trap
pages 55–76.
Copyright © 2024 by Information Age Publishing
www.infoagepub.com
All rights of reproduction in any form reserved.

schooling that have undergirded educational policy debates in the United States and which provide useful background in exploring care in this classroom: 1) the aim of "democratic equality" forefronts the development of citizens; 2) the aim of "social efficiency" prepares students to be workers in a stratified society (i.e., students are prepared for jobs for which they are best suited); and 3) the aim of "social mobility" prepares students to be competitive in the social world (i.e., positioning students to compete for their desired "social positions"). This framework is useful in understanding how the aims of school imply how school ought to be done. Conversely, it follows that what happens on the ground in schools and classrooms actively constructs aims.

The ways in which individuals expressed care in the ELL classroom at WRHS oriented them toward different aims of schooling and cultivated different kinds of citizenship. With closer analysis, these different manifestations of care illuminate whether and how the social actors worked for equity through the project of teaching and learning. Previous chapters have demonstrated that the care in this classroom constructed sanctuary in the space, but an analysis of the kinds of care helps to explore the question of care to what end?

THE STUDENTS: GUIDES ON THE UNDERGROUND RAILROAD

Students manifested care for themselves, their families, their teachers, and each other by helping each other in all kinds of ways and by serving as guides to new students. As students demonstrated care for each other, they also modeled how to navigate and manipulate the structures of schooling, and to stay hidden as they did so. The expressions of care manifested by the students pointed to an aim of hiding—evading the notice of the agents of institutionalized power. While students learned to navigate some of the institutions of society and the school, the degree of their success depended on how well they learned to remain hidden within the school and society. As such, they learned to interrogate the systems of oppression to navigate them for their own survival and benefit, which was a form of disruption, but they did not learn to assert agency in transforming those systems in a more just and sustainable way.

Constructing and Navigating an Underground Railroad

Students in this classroom demonstrated care for each other by serving as guides to new students and members of their classroom and program community—guides to the classroom and school in general, and in constructing and navigating a network of safe spaces, a sort of Underground Railroad. They also gave and accepted help to one another as part of this role. In doing so, they drew upon and built what Tara Yosso (2005) has called "cultural community wealth"— encompassing "aspirational, linguistic, familial, social, and navigational capital" (p. 78)—to help each other navigate their new realities and to imagine futures for themselves. Widening the scope of what kinds of knowledge and experiences

The Implications of Care • 57

"count" in school and society allows an examination of the culturally mediated ways students asserted agency.

Students knew how to find help; at the same time, students' behaviors and movements were policed and they had to find ways to get around the restrictions. Yosso (2005) notes, "Navigational capital [...] acknowledges individual agency within institutional constraints, but it also connects to social networks that facilitate community navigation through places and spaces including schools" (p. 80). To illustrate by example, when the class was learning about the Civil War, I helped Mrs. Sánchez find a translation for the Underground Railroad, and we settled on *El Pasaje Subteráneo* (The Underground Passage). The substitute teacher described the Underground Railroad as "a system that helped slaves escape," and Alejandro looked pensive as he paused his notetaking to observe aloud, "Like the office." The substitute teacher further explained that the Underground Railroad was "a connection of secret places." It occurred to me that the students had their own connection of secret places within the school, and Alejandro's connection to the office as a place that helped people escape indicated that it clearly resonated with some of them as well.

There were other "secret places" in this network, too. They often went to the library to meet up with each other to share answers or just to visit quietly. Students also escaped Mrs. Durham's classroom—often under the pretense of going to the bathroom or to the library—to go to the adjacent empty classroom where they entered quietly and left the lights dim to go unnoticed as they worked together on assignments. Mrs. Durham and Mrs. Sánchez seemed to be aware of the various places to which students might go to get help, and they were often able to head them off by getting there first; at times, they caught students as they were in the process of sharing answers.

New students enrolled in Washington River High School with dizzying frequency. The students in Mrs. Durham's classroom served as guides for the new students, helping them navigate daily life in their new school. Anyelín explained, "We help [the new students], and the teachers tell them how to learn and what they have to do." All students in this classroom could empathize with the feeling of being new. Students all spoke about feelings of alienation and of not fitting in at their new school. The language, the classroom norms, and the group dynamics made them feel, as Isabel observed, "*que no encajaban*," as if they did not fit in, and they expressed relief at having had someone reach out to them to invite them to join.

As guides, the students helped new students open their lockers, showed newcomers how to navigate the lunch line, invited them to eat lunch at their table in the cafeteria, and checked in with new students throughout the day. When I asked Isabel how they know how to help new students, she explained that someone had done the same for her when she was new. She emphasized the importance of *showing* the new student "how classes go and how things in the school are" rather than just telling them. Saraí echoed the importance of walking alongside

58 • LEARNING TO HIDE

newcomers to show them the ropes rather than just telling them what to do, recalling that Anyelín had helped her when she was new: "Anyelín showed me how to go through the lunch line and enter my code...twice...and she explained the rules to me."

As new students grew more comfortable and gained experience in the classroom, they grew into the role of guide as well. Caterín Michelle also named Anyelín as the person who had helped her "learn the ropes" of her new school, and Saraí remembered Caterín Michelle having been her guide when she first arrived. Therefore, Caterín Michelle had been a newcomer and transitioned to guide within the space of only a few months. These relationships continued as more experienced students helped students who had been at WRHS for a shorter time with coursework, translating, and understanding school policies and practices. In this way, students leveraged their various forms of capital to welcome, encourage, and help each other.

Help as a Way of Life

Newcomers sought out help, learned to accept help, and also gave help in various ways. They encountered a range of tasks they needed to do to attend school (i.e., get immunizations and provide transcripts and identification); however, there were things students and their families needed to do as residents of the United States as well. For example, they sought help in securing health insurance, registering for Social Security, and enrolling in the Selective Service. In the absence of a birth certificate, they needed to sign an affidavit confirming their identities; this affidavit needed to be notarized, and since the notary public at the school refused to continue to notarize them, they sought help finding a notary public who would sign for them.

While Mrs. Durham and Mrs. Sánchez worked to provide assistance when they could, the students were actually quite adept at finding help for themselves—whether it was with school-related needs or with situations outside of school. Even on my first day in the classroom (and before I had even been introduced to the students), a student approached me with a question about his math review; he saw me, an adult in the classroom as a resource and did not hesitate to ask me for help. Although students flocked to Mrs. Durham's classroom for help, Sayra admitted that she did not talk much with Mrs. Durham because she would "rather look for somebody that can translate." Indeed, translation was a primary concern for most students, especially those who were enrolled in general education courses. Students who were more proficient in English helped each other when they were available, and when students saw a peer getting help from someone, they would slowly gather around that person to "share" the help.

As willing as they were to give help, most students were also willing to accept help. Anyelín explained that since she had arrived in Washington River, she had accepted help from classmates, teachers, and even complete strangers. I routinely saw the students as guides helping new students in the classroom. One morning,

Alejandro came in and, upon seeing a new student, sat down and talked with him about Mrs. Durham. He acted out what she did when she got angry, placing his hands on his hips and talking loudly. The new student smiled and nodded, and when Alejandro sat back down in his seat, he offered his paper to the new student, suggesting, "Copy?" The student took his paper and started to copy onto his own paper. I noted in my fieldnotes, "*He's teaching the new guy how to get it done.*" It was not necessarily about learning the material so much as about completing the task.

The students—with few exceptions—took care of each other in this classroom, even if they were not new students. Almost unanimously, the students said that they helped each other because that is what "buena gente *(good people)*" do. The ways in which they took care of each other ranged from answering a quick question to providing a place to live. I routinely observed students as they worked together on a test review, leaning across the rows to show each other where to find vocabulary words in their notes or in the book. In another example, Mrs. Durham called on Alejandro to share the answer he wrote on a math worksheet: "Alejandro, what did you write down?" He began, "Eleven," and then looked to another student and asked, "¿Cómo se dice 'menos' *(How do you say 'menos')?*" The other student answered, "Minus," and Alejandro snapped his fingers and his face lit up with recall.

Students took care of each other in things concerning their lives beyond the classroom as well. For example, Mrs. Durham had been worrying all day about finding a student a place to live because his father was in jail and the student was living with an uncle who forced him to pay rent to live with him. She wanted to find a place for this student to live without paying rent. Just before lunch, the third block students were entering the classroom as I was leaving for the day. Mrs. Durham asked two of the students if they could take him in; one, without hesitation, nodded and said, "He can live with us." I was surprised to hear such ready willingness, but in retrospect, it aligned well with the collectivist nature of the students' caring relationships.

As students grew to understand the policies and routines of schooling in the United States, their guidance for newcomer students became more nuanced as they navigated their school experiences. This was especially evident in the experiences of the school-to-career students who routinely translated between monolingual English-speaking teachers and newcomer students, even when they may have preferred other opportunities for the school-to-career experience. Alejandro, due to his more advanced proficiency in English, was able to function as an experienced guide although he had been in the U.S. for only a few months. However, his school and life experiences in his home country of Costa Rica were much more similar to life in the U.S. than the experiences of other newcomers (i.e., students from Guatemala, Honduras, or El Salvador), and his English proficiency and biliteracy accelerated his understanding of his new school.

60 • LEARNING TO HIDE

Culturally-Mediated Care

Students also demonstrated care by drawing on "familial capital" as they navigated their schooling experiences (Yosso, 2005). Yosso (2005) explains that familial capital "engages a commitment to community well being and expands the concept of family to include a more broad understanding of kinship" (p. 79). Students brought to bear in school cultural notions of *respeto* and *educación*, which means their behavior is a representation of their families—a role they take seriously. *Educación* implies courtesy, helpfulness, and comporting oneself in a way appropriate to the place and occasion (Valenzuela, 1999). Caterín Michelle acknowledged that she did not want others to view her siblings in a poor light because of her actions: "No me gustaría que tal vez mirara mal a mis hermanos porque yo mire mal a alguien...o por la forma de quien soy. *(I wouldn't want anybody to look down on my siblings because I wasn't being good to the others...or because the kind of person I am).*" Similarly, they knew that they were members of the ELL program, and as such, it was their responsibility to uphold and project a positive image because it reflected on their peers.

The cultural notion of *respeto* also has deep and complex implications for behavior. Valdés (1996) explains that *respeto* guides interpersonal interactions with individuals based on their roles, which is especially significant in familial relationships. This concept provides guidance in understanding the culture of this classroom because a familial culture was purposefully cultivated among the members. Students, drawing on their cultural understanding of family, transferred the notion of *respeto* into the classroom and program space; in fact, many of them used the word to describe the behaviors they hoped to live out in their daily lives. Jesús asserted, "Respeto de todos. Cuando lo tiene respeto, me van a tener el respeto a mí *(I respect everyone. When we have respect for others, they will have respect for us)."* He explained that because he respected others, it meant that he behaved well. Anyelín noted that elders were deserving of respect, but that also those younger than she because this was key in helping children learn respect. She explained, "Respeto a los chiquitos, así por la respetan, nos respetan *(I respect children, through respecting them, they will respect me.)."*

Given the significance of the notion of *respeto* in the students' lives, I explored how their behaviors and words revealed what *respeto* meant in the everyday. One clear manifestation of *respeto* was that sharing was a daily practice. One student often brought a bag of Doritos that he shared with everyone as he walked around the room visiting with his classmates before class started. Jesús, too, often brought food that he shared with his classmates. One morning he carried a plastic Walmart grocery bag, reaching in and plucking a few red grapes at a time from the package. Others near him reached in and grabbed grapes from the outstretched bag.

Students also routinely shared homework and—less often—test answers. They often worked in groups on worksheets and study guides, and as Sayra explained, "Sometimes we explain them to each other; sometimes we just share the answers." One morning, Saraí even lent her study guide—which she completed during the first block—to a student in the next class, who took it out during second block, showing me and another student his prize. Other times, the sharing was more covert, such as when they shared answers on tests. One day when students had been working on a test for about ten minutes, I noticed Saraí exchange a sideways look with another student. She lifted her paper slightly, and the boy leaned over to look at it more closely. He was clearly looking at her answers while Mrs. Durham took a phone call at her desk. In another example, I observed a student as he went to the front to submit his test and on his way back to his desk, walked behind Isabel and looked at her test; he covertly whispered answers as he walked away. While the testing situation warranted a more surreptitious form of sharing answers, the students nonetheless found ways to do it. The notion of *respeto* helped illuminate the interactions of students within the classroom, and even though most of their behaviors purported to be valued in the district given their focus on being respectful, the students remained in the margins of the school community.

The students transferred the familial capital growing out of the cultural notions of *educación* and *respeto* into their interactions in the classroom and ELL program, acknowledging their roles in supporting and helping one another. Jesús's frequent willingness to share his food illustrated how he regarded his peers much like a family, and Saraí's frequent sharing of answers demonstrated how they were even willing to break rules for what they saw as the good of their peers. Students also drew on the knowledge they had developed as family members when they reciprocated help, either by helping with coursework, translating, or by sharing food, and in their roles as guides to new students.

Care for Inclusion

Newcomer students clearly felt that they were viewed and treated differently, especially when they spoke Spanish. Alejandro articulated how he felt others viewed him in the school; he explained in a note to me, "Cuando la gente mira que hablas español te queda biendo raro como si tuvieras un gran moco en la cara *(When people see that you speak Spanish, they keep looking at you strangely, as if you had a big booger on your face.)*." Clearly, he felt that being a Spanish speaker wrought prejudice and discrimination.

Students deliberately reached out to include one another in spaces where they did not experience belonging, such as the school cafeteria. Sayra explained, "There's some days, every time we sit down, we're just a little Hispanic group. Some of them even have talked about they had to sit in a group where some white kids were sitting and the other kids just stood up and basically left the table, so that's why it's weird. I haven't had the experience to see it, but they say that happens." She sensed that she (and other "Hispanics") were not welcome in places where the "white kids" had already laid claim. Sayra was particularly adept at critiquing the structures that privileged English, and she noted, "Tienes que hablar inglés para conocer a las gringas *(You have to speak English in order to be friends with the 'gringas.')*." She used the word "gringas" to refer to white girls who speak English; it is notable that she held no expectation that *las gringas* ought to learn Spanish to be friends with *her*. Even though she had not seen for herself this phenomenon in which white kids left a table when Hispanic kids sat down, this story was part of the lore of belonging for her. An important part of that lore was the lesson to be inclusive of her "Hispanic" peers.

Students' citizenship practices manifested through their care, then, were twofold: one, they taught one another to navigate oppressive institutional structures and spaces in a way that was unobtrusive and unassuming; and two, they taught one another that they mattered and belonged—but only in certain spaces. In this way, newcomers learned that they were valued members of the ELL classroom, but not necessarily so outside of it. They did not experience belonging in the school overall. Rather, they learned that their belonging was qualified on occupying only those spaces to which they had been assigned, and they relied on each other to make those spaces inclusive.

MRS. SÁNCHEZ: CARE AS A CULTURAL PRACTICE

Mrs. Sánchez served as a "cultural broker" (Gentemann & Whitehead, 1983) by drawing on her own experiences to help newcomers navigate new systems and demonstrated "culturally relevant care" (Watson et al., 2016) as she critiqued the positioning of immigrants in the U.S. She also demonstrated characteristics of what Ware (2006) calls a "warm demander" as she held high expectations for students and employed "tough love" to promote students' persistence and perseverance in school. Taken together, her work was oriented toward preparing students to be critical democratic citizens because she modeled a critique of oppressive societal conditions and quietly encouraged students to exercise their rights to transform them.

Cultural Brokering

Mrs. Sánchez, culturally familiar with the students' lives and identities, demonstrated care for students in multiple ways. Gentemann and Whitehead (1983) define cultural brokers as "bicultural actors" who are able to navigate "both cultures, to take mainstream values and communicate them to the ethnic cultures, and communicate the ethnic culture to the mainstream" (p. 119). Mrs. Sánchez served as a cultural broker in many ways similar to how the students served as guides to one another, but she also leveraged her position of authority to help students and their families learn and navigate WRHS and the institution of school in the United States.

She was the first institutional representative most new Spanish-speaking students and families met at WRHS; thus, she played an important role in helping families understand the expectations for school entrance and the process for obtaining transcripts from previous schools. Mrs. Sánchez's role as cultural broker also helped bridge families and the school by fielding attendance phone calls, explaining registration procedures and guidelines between guidance counselors and the students, and translating between administrators or teachers and students when necessary. In this way, she provided access to the parts of WRHS that assumed English proficiency and a cultural understanding of U.S. schooling.

Mrs. Sánchez also helped students understand systems outside the classroom and school. Many students were working to get their residence cards with help from an immigration attorney, and they often brought in correspondence to Mrs. Sánchez to seek help in understanding it. For example, one morning a student brought paperwork in an envelope to Mrs. Sánchez and asked for her help understanding it. She took out the paper, disposing of the envelope in the trashcan next to her desk. Mrs. Sánchez glanced at the envelope and told the student to keep the envelope so that she would have the postmark date documented, and the student bent down to fish it out of the trash can. Mrs. Sánchez pointed to the corner of the envelope to show her where the date was on the envelope and the student nodded in understanding. Mrs. Sánchez knew that keeping the envelope was important in proving dates received, should the need to do that arise. The student learned an important lesson in self-advocacy with a small, but powerful teaching moment.

Students recognized that Mrs. Sánchez was a resource for cultural brokering. Saraí noted that Mrs. Sánchez gave them help with a number of things; she explained, "Nos ayuda en los trabajos cuando no entendemos y nos explica *(She helps us with our work when we don't understand and she explains it)."* Sayra echoed this, adding that Mrs. Sánchez is a resource outside the classroom as well, "Pues, si necesitaramos como hablar en la oficina o con otras cosas en la escuela *(Like, if we need her for how to talk in the office or with other things in the school)."* Mrs. Sánchez even accompanied five students and another ELL teacher on an out-of-town college visit.

Mrs. Sánchez was also a role model as a cultural broker. She modeled learning as she continued to learn Spanish vocabulary and spelling, and she frequently mentioned facts or ideas that were important to know in relation to pursuing U.S. citizenship, such as when she emphasized the importance of knowing that George Washington was the first U.S. president. Relatedly, she validated and affirmed students' efforts in class, especially when they volunteered responses to questions about course content. She also modeled the role of an advocate as a professional within the school and classroom, watching out for fairness in disciplinary actions (such as when she followed through on her word by defending students when she had granted permission to use their phones) and accuracy in translations.

At the same time that Mrs. Sánchez was a support to students, she was clearly not a "friend" to them; she described herself as "more strict" than others in her position (paraeducator) at the school. Just a look from Mrs. Sánchez could silence or change the behavior of even the most rambunctious of the students. She policed students in the school and in the classroom, such as when she commented on Isabel's shirt being too short because it showed a few inches of her belly and explained that it was in violation of the student code of conduct outlined in the

64 • LEARNING TO HIDE

handbook. Certainly, it is oppressive that young women's bodies are policed in school (and in society), but by sharing *why* the shirt was problematic she was able to alert Isabel to the fact that her body *is* policed. Policing their behaviors was a way of teaching the "mainstream culture" to newcomers.

The students and their families trusted Mrs. Sánchez in her role as a cultural broker. They viewed her as an advocate and someone who could help them navigate their new realities in the United States. This is perhaps why her policing of their bodies and behaviors felt less threatening; instead, they viewed her policing as well-intentioned advice. The students' willingness to talk with her about their daily lives *and* respond to her as an authority figure demonstrated the authentic caring relationship (Valenzuela, 1999) between them.

Culturally Relevant Care

Mrs. Sánchez demonstrated what Watson et al. (2016) call "culturally relevant care," going beyond traditional notions of care to include "genuine recognition of each other's wholeness and being able to identify with each other's experiences" (p. 999). Because her identities and experiences so closely mirrored those of the students in the classroom and because she acted as a cultural broker, Mrs. Sánchez was able to cultivate trusting relationships with them and at the same time model critical practices of democratic citizenship, such as critiquing and resisting stratifying and oppressive policies and practices.

Mrs. Sánchez's high expectations for what students ought to know to navigate American life manifested culturally relevant care. She could empathize with and model what it meant to be a Person of Color, an immigrant, and a Latinx woman in the school world and in life. For example, she resisted the substitute teacher's low expectation that students learn the umbrella term, "Congress" and not learn the names of the two houses of Congress, and insisted, "They need to know it."

Mrs. Sánchez also knew the importance of encouraging the young women in the class to speak with confidence in their abilities, especially academically. Her quiet verbal observation of the number of female volunteers in the class, "Las mujeres están dominando el día de hoy *(The women are dominating today.),*" was a message to the young people in the class that the women were intelligent and capable, and even leaders. Her own cultural life experiences had reinforced the expectation that Latinx women be submissive and deferent to men. In this way, she acknowledged cultural understanding and, viewing it as oppressive in her own life, disrupted it at the same time.

Mrs. Sánchez's translation and interpretation in Mrs. Durham's classroom expanded and enriched the content of the curriculum for students. She leveraged her experiences of learning English as she identified what to take apart and on what to elaborate and enrich. Sayra acknowledged that Mrs. Sánchez explained the content in more detail, noting, "There are things that we understand but in a short version and [Mrs. Sánchez] kind of extends it and explains it to us better.

The Implications of Care • 65

She gives us more details." She did this by providing background information and scaffolding vocabulary development.

Mrs. Sánchez leveraged her experience of learning English in her translation work with students. Sometimes she would translate exactly what Mrs. Durham or other teachers said, but other times she added details or offered an alternate word. She explained, "We have kids that haven't had any previous schooling, so if [Mrs. Durham] says something about like 'the sum' of this number, I know they're not gonna understand what 'the sum' means. So I try to go more in detail." She continued, "if *I* can't really understand it in English, I mean I understand English, but if I can't figure it out myself, I know they're probably not going to be able to figure it out, so I try to explain it to them more." Mrs. Sánchez knew well the experience of needing more clarity or even simple rephrasing, and this experience allowed her to see and address the same needs in the students.

The bulk of Mrs. Sánchez's work in translating was in the course of the daily activities of the ELL classroom. She explained: "For the whole class, Mrs. Durham—she says her lesson in English and then I just interpret it in Spanish so the kids can understand, or even when the kids need to ask her a question and they don't know how to ask her, I interpret that for them."

This was a rather simplistic description of what was actually a very complex task. Mrs. Durham and Mrs. Sánchez had a practiced lesson routine in which Mrs. Durham read, paused for Mrs. Sánchez to translate, projected a slide of notes in English that she also read, and again waited for Mrs. Sánchez to translate; the students then copied the notes from the slide.

The day when Mrs. Durham introduced their new unit aimed at helping students understand elections and political parties in the United States in the two weeks leading up to the 2016 election provides a useful demonstration of the complexity of the Mrs. Sánchez's translation work in class lessons. Mrs. Durham introduced students to the Democratic and Republican political parties in the United States, and briefly discussed the occasional strong third-party candidate. She directed them to the ISideWith.com website which allows a person to make selections based on their values and views on a range of social, economic, and environmental issues, and then it tabulates to which presidential candidate their responses most closely align. They worked together through the questions offered in English. The topics ran the gamut of our shared societal lives. How did they feel about Affirmative Action, "decriminalization" of drugs? Should presidential candidates be required to release their tax returns? I was in awe of how Mrs. Sánchez expanded the explanations so that students understood the possible responses offered; she had to draw on a range of background knowledge to translate these real issues.

Mrs. Sánchez took on the task of explaining some deeply thorny and nuanced issues; most of these questions assumed background knowledge—at least having heard of the issue—and Mrs. Sánchez built that knowledge as she translated. The translation here went beyond merely providing students with the Spanish words

66 • LEARNING TO HIDE

for what they were reading; she wanted them to understand what these unfamiliar concepts and diverse perspectives were. Mrs. Sánchez's task in this lesson was daunting and complicated, but she helped them construct understanding of these very real issues by going beyond mere literal translation to offer them a conceptual explanation.

Mrs. Sánchez explained to me that she knew many students were trying to get their residence status, so she tried to add information about the systems and structures in the United States—including privileged knowledge—based on her own experiences that would help them in that process. I observed that she added in subtle details and cues when she translated, such as when Mrs. Durham asked about who George Washington was. When Alejandro asked, "He is on the dollar bill?" Mrs. Sánchez confirmed that and added that they should know that for the citizenship test. I asked her why she decided to add that information, and she explained, "It just comes to me 'cause I'm working on eventually getting [U.S. residence]. And I think knowing who the first president was is very important." She took advantage of the tiny moments in which she could add this important teaching, and the teaching was based in her own experience.

She also added information that was relevant to their lives, thereby connecting the curriculum to their lived experiences, as when she explained due process as it related to immigration cases or reminded students in the wake of Trump's election that "Americans" would probably not do the work immigrants were doing in meatpacking plants and trailer washes. The morning when Mrs. Durham asked students to write their concerns about how the 2016 election would affect their lives, Mrs. Sánchez translated between the teacher and the students. One group of students asked, "Will the Americans replace the jobs of Hispanics?" Before Mrs. Durham responded, Mrs. Sánchez interjected spitefully, "Nobody's gonna go work with the pigs at Hormel," and there was agreement all around that no "Americans" would choose to do the work immigrants did in the meatpacking plants in Washington River. Students also wondered whether visas would be canceled, and Mrs. Sánchez explained due process to them when Mrs. Durham was at a loss for how to explain it. Mrs. Sánchez, it was clear, knew the process too well. For this work, she leveraged her experiences as an immigrant and a language learner to know what was relevant to students' lives.

The Warm Demander

Mrs. Sánchez built caring relationships with the students in the classroom. She supported their needs, learned about their backgrounds, and connected with them through humor and teasing; she also used tough love with the students when necessary. When I asked the students about their relationship with Mrs. Sánchez, Caterín Michelle noted that she felt Mrs. Sánchez was a good person, and that "nos apoya bastante...siempre *(she supports us so much...always)."* Anyelín said over and over that Mrs. Sánchez had helped her in so many ways, and it was clear that she felt Mrs. Sánchez cared for her. "Me ayuda mucho—con mis tareas, y me

The Implications of Care • 67

ayudó a buscar trabajo también *(She helps me a lot—with my homework, and she helped me look for a job too)."*

Mrs. Sánchez sometimes adopted a sterner demeanor when dealing with students; this was a noticeable change from her gentle and caring personality. When she sensed that a student was trying to make her feel sorry for him or her, or that the student was wallowing in self-pity, she changed how she interacted with them. She explained, "When the kids tell me, 'You know, I'm gonna drop out. I don't wanna go back to school.' The first thing I tell them is, 'You have to stay in school. It's either school or go work somewhere where you're not gonna like the job.' And I always tell them, 'You know, you just have to...either way, you have to get your education and think about yourself first.' I think they need to hear that from somebody else that's not their guardians or their parents."

She admitted that there was a point at which she changed her response to students who continued to threaten to "drop out" of school. She would feign acceptance of their decision, saying, "Okay. Tell me when and I'll fill out the applications. Just turn in your books and you can just leave." Typically, the student would react in surprise and ask, "You're not gonna tell me that I have to stay?" to which she would respond, "No, because you're always telling me this. If you really wanna do that, if you really want your life to change that way, then I'm not gonna be the one that's telling you stay if next thing you know you're gonna be like, 'I'm leaving again.' If you want to, just tell me when and we can do it." Again pretending to be disinterested, she added, "But, just so you know, we're working on your transcripts, and we might get you to another grade higher, but if you're gonna leave just tell me and I will stop doing that 'cause I took so much time yesterday to do that."

She reflected about why students approached her with their threats to leave school, observing, "I think sometimes they just wanna ask my attention and I think they want us to be sorry for them. But I think sometimes they need somebody to just be like, 'Okay. Do whatever you want, but you know, this is gonna happen, this is gonna change.' That normally makes them stay." This form of "tough love" was important in encouraging students to stay in school; she seemed to know just when to offer them a little kernel of hope that they were making progress and would be able to finish high school.

As discussed earlier, Mrs. Sánchez was a teacher in all ways but credentials as she provided access to and enriched the curriculum. In comparison to Mrs. Durham (and the substitute teachers they had), she held higher expectations for what students should and could learn. Caterín Michelle certainly valued Mrs. Sánchez, asserting that "if it weren't for Mrs. Sánchez, we wouldn't learn *anything."* She created opportunities for students to understand the material more deeply and to be someone they could ask when they had questions. Mrs. Sánchez opened these opportunities by expanding on or breaking down what Mrs. Durham said—usually by connecting ideas to students' lives, rephrasing questions, affirming stu-

68 • LEARNING TO HIDE

dents' responses, and creating space for students to ask questions. In this way, her translation and interpretation were their own form of teaching.

Mrs. Sánchez often added information into what Mrs. Durham said; in this way, she connected the curriculum to students' lives. One example of this was when they were studying women's suffrage. Mrs. Durham summarized as she projected the slide, "Now in America, anyone over 18 can vote." Mrs. Sánchez translated that and then added, "as long as they are American citizens." Clearly, this was relevant and meaningful information in these students' lives. Not *anyone* over 18 can vote in the United States, and many of these students were among them.

Sayra explained that Mrs. Sánchez enriched an otherwise simple curriculum, which afforded them access to information and more "details" about what they were learning. She said, "There are things that we understand but in a short version and [Mrs. Sánchez] kind of prolongs it and explains it to us better. She gives us more details. We understand Mrs. Durham but there are certain words that when Mrs. Sanchez explains it better we're like, 'Ah! Yes, we understand what she's trying to say now.'" Sayra valued the extra information Mrs. Sánchez made accessible to them.

Sayra gave an example of how Mrs. Sánchez helped in class, explaining: "Es difícil cuando nosotros queremos hacer comentario a que la maestra pregunte *(It's difficult when we want to make a comment about what the teacher asks),"* but "Mrs. Sánchez nos ayuda traducir lo que queremos decir, y pues, es fácil porque nos ayuda Mrs. Sánchez *(Mrs. Sánchez helps us translate what we want to say, and well, it's easy because Mrs. Sánchez helps us)."* Sayra felt that Mrs. Sánchez created space for her intelligence to be recognized; Mrs. Sánchez allowed for Sayra's and others' voices and thoughts to be heard.

Mrs. Sánchez also validated students' learning when they volunteered answers to questions in class. One morning, Mrs. Sánchez's affirming support of Alejandro's answer did much to tamp down the dubious reaction of the substitute teacher. In response to the question, "What is ratification?" Alejandro gave the correct answer in Spanish. Mrs. Sánchez translated, and the teacher praised him. "Woohoo!" he says with a smirk and a brief pump of his fist. The teacher asked the next question, and Mrs. Sánchez translated it, reading from Alejandro's paper over his shoulder. Alejandro offered an answer in Spanish to her, and she told him he was correct. When he volunteered the answer to the teacher, the teacher said jokingly, "She told you!" gesturing toward Mrs. Sánchez. Mrs. Sánchez shook her head adamantly, insisting, "No! He knew it!" Alejandro did not seem to react to the sub's teasing accusation, but I was affronted by it. So many non-Spanish speakers tend to assume that something covert is happening when people speak Spanish together, and I was frustrated that this was yet another microaggression they had to tolerate in school. I was thankful that Mrs. Sánchez had been so supportive, and I hoped that was what would stay with him.

Mrs. Sánchez demonstrated care in the classroom as a cultural broker, a warm demander, and through culturally relevant care. She acted as a bridge between the students and their teachers, the school, and the community, and she supported students as they worked toward a high school diploma—which sometimes required tough love. She did, however, help them to see and critique the way they were positioned within the school and society. Although she did not explicitly describe her stance as oriented toward social justice, she fostered an understanding of the stratified and hierarchical society in the U.S. and encouraged them to push back against it. In these ways, Mrs. Sánchez perhaps modeled for newcomers the most critical practices of citizenship.

MRS. DURHAM: CARE FOR SURVIVAL

Mrs. Durham's care for students was motivated by good intentions to help students navigate their new realities. She cared about and for her students, but regardless of intentions, the ways in which she sheltered them (e.g., discouraging them from discussing politics and insisting that they come to her for help) were aimed at protecting them from the injustices in society and evaded possibilities for disrupting systems of oppression at their roots. This maintained the status quo of the systems within which immigrants are problematized, criminalized, and marginalized. In addition, because Mrs. Durham privileged English learning over content knowledge, students did not have opportunities for deep critical learning about how they were positioned in U.S. history or the collective nature of social justice movements. As such, Mrs. Durham's care fostered a conceptualization of citizenship in which they relied on others to transform inequities while they merely survived on the margins. This care prompts questions about the structures and systems that create and sustain the conditions in which she felt compelled to protect students.

Triage for Assessment of Needs

Mrs. Durham worked exceedingly hard to meet students' needs and to help them feel welcome in the school. However, the ways in which she demonstrated care were not necessarily aimed toward helping them gain independence. She coordinated help within the school and community, and she thrived on serving her students. She enjoyed the gifts and gestures of appreciation students bestowed upon her. She wished to be understood as different from other teachers, allowing students special privileges—like listening to music or using their phones—in her classroom that other teachers did not permit. Mrs. Durham was also the gatekeeper for communications between students and the world outside her classroom, which meant that she decided what information students received.

Mrs. Durham diagnosed and helped newcomer students with a range of needs. Her classroom was like a triage in which she assessed students' needs and the severity of them before she acted. She prioritized the direst needs and documented

70 • LEARNING TO HIDE

those that could wait. Considered most urgent were issues of housing and food security; making appointments with eye doctors or dentists were usually (but not always) less urgent and could be postponed if needed. She admitted that although her official role was to teach students English, she felt more strongly about the ways in which she could help students learn survival skills for life in the U.S.

Mrs. Durham was a resource for nearly everything: obtaining health insurance, scheduling immunizations, securing copies of birth certificates, finding notaries for families who signed affidavits in lieu of providing a birth certificate, registering for Selective Service, obtaining a social security number, and finding jobs and money. Even former students came to her for help. She often used her own money and resources to provide for her students, and she made the classroom space homey and welcoming to students. Students valued and appreciated her help, but her help often positioned the students and their families to need and depend on her rather than equipping them with the knowledge and skills to navigate societal institutions themselves.

Fostering Sanctuary

Mrs. Durham's classroom was a space that was comfortable and flexible, offering students comfortable places to sit, food and drinks for purchase, and frequent opportunities to listen to music and enjoy some free time. Humor and silliness were part of the culture of the room, and it was clear that students were comfortable and safe there. The comfort and safety students experienced in this sanctuary-like space were especially relevant to their lives outside of school, in which discussions of "sanctuary" had real-life implications for their security from authorities with deportation orders. Even authorized immigrants felt anxious and insecure in the context of Trump's threats of mass deportations.

Mrs. Durham demonstrated care in her interpersonal relationships with students, complimenting their haircuts or new glasses. She also acknowledged that most of her students' life situations did not fit well within the structure of school, and therefore, bent rules (i.e., allowing cell phones at appropriate times) to make it possible for students to navigate school while serving as an interpreter for a parent or as a caretaker for a younger sibling. She also rewarded students with parties and tokens that students could submit to a drawing for prizes when they demonstrated behaviors that were valued by the school and mainstream society (i.e., being "safe," being "respectful," and being "responsible").[2] She claimed that so many of her students "did not have childhoods," so she worked to give them what she thought of as childhood experiences. The newcomers did, in fact, have childhoods; their childhoods were just not what she imagined or acknowledged as a childhood.

---

[2] This reward system was a part of the schoolwide Positive Behavioral Intervention and Supports (PBIS) model for behavior management. See more about PBIS at https://www.pbis.org/pbis/what-is-pbis.

The Implications of Care • 71

To offer students what she saw as a childhood experience, Mrs. Durham arranged for the students to raise money for a day trip to an area zoo in the spring. She distributed order forms and explained that they would be selling tee shirts and hoodies as a fundraiser to earn money for the trip. The EL program sold shirts once a year for fundraising purposes, but that year's shirts were different. She explained proudly: "For the first time since I've been here, we will be selling shirts with Spanish on them. This is the first time we've had Spanish on shirts." That year's design represented the school colors—gray with gold writing. The front read, "Hear Us, See Us," above the school name and mascot, the words shaped into a tiger paw to symbolize the school mascot. On the back the lines alternated between Spanish and English, reading:

ESE MOMENTO *(THAT MOMENT)*
WHEN YOU START
PENSANDO EN *(THINKING IN)*
DOS IDIOMAS *(TWO LANGUAGES)*
AT THE SAME
TIEMPO *(TIME)*

Mrs. Durham explained what sizes and styles of shirts and hoodies were available and how to fill out the order forms, and she wrote the prices on the board while Mrs. Sánchez translated and clarified the information—adding a description of what a fundraiser was.

Students inquired about the trip to the zoo, asking when and who would go. Mrs. Durham responded that they would take the trip "sometime in the spring," and that only those students who sold three shirts would be able to go on the trip. Most (but not all) students were moderately excited about the prospect of a day out of school, and the trip to this zoo was indeed one that all the district's students enjoyed as a field trip during their elementary school years, although elementary school students did not have to conduct fundraisers to be able to go. Having arrived in Washington River as high school students, Mrs. Durham wished for her students to have the experience as well.

Offering Support

Mrs. Durham also demonstrated care in more symbolically supportive ways. For example, on the morning following Trump's election, she took time to reassure students that Trump would not alone have the power to rule. She joked that students could come and live in her basement if necessary; while they all giggled at that invitation and joked about it in the days to come, the idea that they would be safe from deportation (or from racism more generally) in her basement was misguided and false. Similarly, her advice to students that they come to her if they felt threatened or experienced racist attacks—while born of good intentions—

72 • LEARNING TO HIDE

conveyed that she could save them from the attacks, or at the very least, seek out consequences for perpetrators.

Another symbolic gesture of care Mrs. Durham demonstrated was her occasional effort to learn phrases in the students' languages. Students taught her short phrases that were relevant to what they were doing or phrases they said often, but she learned them playfully with no earnest attempt at being able to communicate with students and their families in their dominant languages. So, while it was fun to play with the language—learning rhymes and playful phrases like "I love you"—Mrs. Durham spoke English almost all the time. When pressed because of Mrs. Sánchez's absence or when another translator was unavailable, she attempted to thread Spanish words into her communication with students, and for the most part, students understood enough to rely on the more experienced English learners to translate for them.

Mrs. Durham was exceedingly patient, especially when it came to allowing students time to acculturate to their new classroom when they first arrived in Washington River. She understood that newcomers needed time to trust her, and she allowed them as much time as they needed. She had faith, though, that her students would indeed come to trust her: "I know they feel safe in the room when they start coming to me for help. When they come to *me* to ask a question instead of maybe a [paraeducator] or another student. I think it helps the kids see how other kids have built a relationship with me and so the kids talk and they know." She trusted that they would, in time, accept their position in the "family tree" of her classroom.

Mrs. Durham's ever-present humor infused the room with laughter and provided levity in darker moments, which was an aspect of the support she offered. Taking a cue from her students, she was also able to make light of situations that were unfair or frustrating, and together, they found humor in the mishaps and misunderstandings that occur with language development. One such instance occurred when Mrs. Durham used an idiom and a student who generally understood most of what Mrs. Durham said in English looked at her blankly: Mrs. Durham walked to a student, who was sitting in a chair next to Mrs. Sánchez and reminded him he needed to be in his seat. "I no talk here but my desk yes!" he protested. "When pigs fly!" she retorted. The student stared blankly at her, not having understood the idiom, and then they all laughed. Mrs. Sánchez explained the idiom in between giggles, and the student laughed as he listened. Mrs. Durham laughed delightedly when she used phrases that seemed to her students so nonsensical. Their ability to laugh about the absurdity of such phrases gave them meaningful moments to refer back to as they learned.

Mrs. Durham aimed to make her students feel good about themselves, and to that end, gave them frequent compliments on a range of things from haircuts to good work in class. She sat at her desk one day and began calling attendance. "Mario?" she called. "Sí," he answered quietly. She looked up at him and pointing to her hair, said, "Me gusta *(I like)* your haircut." Mario smiled and smoothed his

The Implications of Care • 73

hair as he looked down at his desk sheepishly. In another example, Mrs. Durham was walking to her desk and paused beside a male student and gestured to his new glasses. "Mucho guapo," she said, intending to communicate, "very handsome," although the literal translation was "much handsome." He knew what she meant, and he smiled and nodded back at her.

Mrs. Durham also complimented their academic successes, particularly when she knew they had worked hard to achieve the expectations. For example, she was excited to share with them the results of their standardized test scores for reading. "EVERYONE raised their scores! One person even raised her score by 700 points!" The students cheered and looked around to see if they could identify who had earned such a jump in her score. Mrs. Durham also wrote encouraging messages on sticky notes she attached to their submitted assignments before returning them. Students could then add their note to the class's collection on a bulletin board at the back of the room; the class that accumulated the most notes by the end of each nine-week quarter earned a party. These small celebrations bolstered students' pride in their accomplishments and encouraged them to work as a class to collect the most notes.

Structure and Routine

Mrs. Durham also provided structure, an important element of sanctuary (Antrop-González, 2003; Bloom, 2005). She insisted that students know the school and classroom rules, and she enforced them. One persistent problem she encountered was students arriving tardy to school. Students who arrived after the tardy bell had to visit the attendance clerk in the main office to get a pink tardy pass that served as a pass to their first class and that indicated the thirty minutes the student was obliged to serve after school as the consequence for having arrived late. Mrs. Durham, although she understood very well the number of circumstances that could cause students to be late, enforced this school policy consistently.

Mrs. Durham also insisted that students take care of the physical space of the classroom. She provided comfortable chairs and side tables that infused the space with a touch of home, and she did not allow students to abuse these items. When three students were teasingly pushing each other and one fell onto the low-lying coffee table positioned in front of the sofa, she refrained from lecturing them on classroom behavior, and instead, she told the three students they would be staying after school to fix the table. Other times, she shouted, "Move your nalgas *(butt)*!" when too many students piled into a chair. She reminded them that they needed to take care of the furniture if they wished to have those seating options.

There were many times that I described Mrs. Durham in my notes as a "watchdog" (Viesca & Gray, 2021). She was constantly on the watch for students who were breaking the rules. Sometimes she dutifully enforced the consequences of the rule-breaking when they involved communication with the administrative office, but other times she handled the offenses herself. The use of cell phones for music or videos during instruction, for example, almost always resulted in Mrs.

74 • LEARNING TO HIDE

Durham confiscating the phones and taking them to the office, where the students would be able to pick them up after school with no further consequence.

Most often, however, Mrs. Durham handled disciplinary issues on her own—directly and simply. One morning, the students were chatting quietly as they waited for the school bell to sound. Mrs. Durham was outside the classroom in the hallway, and her voice suddenly rose above the quiet din in the classroom as she entered with a student. "And you! No más skipping school!" The student had posted photos of himself with his girlfriend on the day he skipped school; he had previously added Mrs. Durham as a friend on Facebook, so she saw the post. When Mrs. Durham walked away, he whispered to a friend sitting nearby, asking about which photos she had seen. Apparently, the girl with whom he spent the "skipped days" had tagged him in a photo, alerting Mrs. Durham to see what he was doing those days. She had communicated with a simple stern message that the student had been caught. The student heeded this warning and was present for the rest of the week.

There were numerous students who came to Mrs. Durham's classroom for assistance with assignments and tests from other classes. Mrs. Durham collaborated with the general education classroom teachers to understand which accommodations she could provide (i.e., defining words, reading the questions aloud to the student, etc.), as the students often misinformed her when they came to her room. One morning, Mrs. Durham listened dubiously to two students insisting they could use their notes on the exam they brought with them. Mrs. Durham took their test papers to the hallway and called to catch the other teacher in the hallway to ask about accommodations. The students ran to the other classroom door to eavesdrop on the teachers' discussion, and they listened and exchanged worried glances with each other. Mrs. Durham returned to the classroom, and when she told the students that they could not use their notes, their shoulders fell.

The structure Mrs. Durham provided, though, was tempered with her acknowledgement of students' realities and their individual needs; sometimes, this meant that the rules needed to be subverted, dismissed, or broken. Most often, students were granted a temporary pass on the rule that students could not use cell phones in class. For example, when Saraí's phone buzzed while the students worked on an assignment independently, she walked quickly to Mrs. Durham and told her who was calling. Mrs. Durham nodded her approval, and Saraí took the call. Mrs. Durham's nod signaled her acknowledgement that the student's need to take the phone call was greater than the rule that stated she could not use it.

Mrs. Durham's roles as the helper, the supporter, and the provider of structure were focused on making school a place where students felt safe, secure, and cared for. Her efforts were oriented toward building relationships with students, but her efforts yielded relationships that were more utilitarian. Schooling structures and policies constructed the paradoxical tension between being supportive to students and surveilling them, which proved difficult to navigate. While relationships were clearly important in Mrs. Durham's classroom, they were quite separate from the

The Implications of Care • 75

learning they did about American history, and the message was clear that school *outside* of this classroom was not a welcoming space. Thus, students learned to depend on someone else—someone positioned with more institutional power—to make change. While they were protected in this classroom, they were also not taught how to democratically act to transform the oppressive structures and practices of school.

CARE TO WHAT END?

The ways in which the students, Mrs. Sánchez, and Mrs. Durham demonstrated care in this classroom were oriented toward different aims of schooling and different conceptions of citizenship. This prompts a necessary interrogation of care. Care to what end? This question is especially important because of the important role that school plays as a public space for newcomers. The social actors in the space navigated a power-laden system that positioned them differently based on their roles.

As the students helped each other to navigate the school in a way that allowed them to "play the game" of the institution that was dismissive of their presence, they worked toward an aim of evasion—learning to map the safe spaces within the school while also remaining unnoticed. This taught them that staying hidden and evading notice was how they could thrive as citizens. This was and is incredibly problematic in a sociopolitical context in which immigrants and migrants have been systemically criminalized (i.e., through policies and the associated rhetoric labeling them as "legal" or "illegal") and marginalized (i.e., by placement in detention camps and in this case, in ELL classrooms). To both acknowledge the U.S.'s complicity in creating the conditions that drive immigration *and* to live out the ideals of the Constitution's promise of freedom and justice for all, all citizens must hear them and see them as human beings worthy of dignity and human rights.

Mrs. Sánchez, through culturally relevant care and her roles as a cultural broker and a warm demander, oriented her work toward the critical practices of transformative democratic citizenship, fostering a sense of belonging for students. This cultivated citizenship practices aimed at speaking truths about their realities and critiquing structures that were exclusive of them and others like them. Mrs. Sánchez's culturally mediated citizenship also modeled how to claim space and rights within the institutionalized structures that systemically marginalize newcomers, but also how to leverage the rights and responsibilities of citizenship in the U.S. to transform the practices of their own cultures that they experience as oppressive (Flores, 2003; Flores & Benmayor, 1997).

Finally, while Mrs. Durham's care came from a place of deep care, it was oriented toward an aim of survival by tacit acceptance of a position within society's already stratified structure. Mrs. Durham's intentions were certainly motivated by great care, but her care perpetuated students' dependence on her rather than helping them claim independence and assert agency on their own behalf. This care was rooted in her understanding of the oppressive policies and practices from which she was trying to protect students, the policies and practices in which she was complicit. Again, the institutionalized policies warrant interrogation over the well-intentioned educators confronting ethical dilemmas in their daily work.

As I have said, newcomer students certainly need a sanctuary space to make sense of their new realities and to construct healthy and vibrant hybrid identities, and also to claim respite from the incessant messages that serve to pathologize their existence. As a space filled with laughter and love, students undoubtedly learned to care for each other in this classroom, and they learned important citizenship practices that positioned them to critique and push back against oppressive policies and practices. However, because the sanctuary isolated them from their fellow citizens, the critical citizenship practices they learned were contained within the margins of their classroom. The sanctuary, thus, became a trap.

CHAPTER 6

MISSED OPPORTUNITIES IN THE CLASSROOM AND SCHOOL

School mission statements often highlight commitments to equity and inclusion, but the efficacy of these statements is debatable. The arrival of newcomer students to a school most certainly prompts some growing pains; however, Washington River High School's response to newcomer students was more focused on fitting students into the extant structure of the school than on transforming itself to integrate newcomers' lives. There were a number of missed opportunities to integrate newcomers into the classroom, the curriculum, and the daily life of WRHS. As such, the school and actors within it evaded opportunities to address inequities, to position newcomers as agents of transforming inequities, and to foster belonging in the school and community.

What I viewed as opportunities were regarded by the school as problems or sometimes overlooked altogether. First, the school dismissed students' multilinguistic skills in Spanish and languages indigenous to Guatemala (i.e., K'iche', Mam, Q'anjob'al) as a deficiency in English. The school did not acknowledge their linguistic funds of knowledge (González et al., 2005; Moll et al., 1992) *unless* these skills could be deployed to translate. Second, there were missed opportunities in the sheltered U.S. history class to integrate newcomers into the national narrative, evading opportunities to explore counternarratives to the majoritarian

---

Learning to Hide: The English Learning Classroom as Sanctuary and Trap
pages 77–86.
Copyright © 2024 by Information Age Publishing
www.infoagepub.com
All rights of reproduction in any form reserved.

78 • LEARNING TO HIDE

stories of U.S. history. Third, there were missed opportunities to integrate civic education, especially following Trump's election when students had to grapple to understand a new life in the U.S. and simultaneously make sense of life in America in a Trump administration. Finally, there were missed opportunities to include newcomer students in the school community beyond the walls of the ELL hallway and to foster social interactions in the society-building micromoments of school. These represented multiple missed opportunities for a more deliberate cultivation of democratic citizenship to foster belonging in the wider school and community.

Missed Opportunities to Draw Out and Leverage Students' Funds of Knowledge

Newcomer students to WRHS came to school with funds of knowledge (González et al., 2005; Moll et al., 1992) learned through their experiences in their home countries, on their journeys to the U.S. and Washington River, and in the brief time they had lived in Washington River. Students had developed proficient linguistic skills in one or more languages; almost all students from Guatemala spoke at least two languages. Most students had attended school—many with gaps and interruptions in formal schooling—in their home countries, and thus, held understandings of schooling and other forms of education. The ways in which newcomers made their way to the U.S. and to Washington River varied, but the knowledge they learned and practiced during their journeys "al Norte" provided opportunities to connect new learning to these experiences.

Students' deficiency in English was centered as soon as they enrolled in WRHS and were labeled "English Language Learners (ELLs)." The goal of learning English was forefronted through this placement, especially because it comprised the majority of their school day. Students took "sheltered" content courses during the first part of the day, then took a full block of "ELL," focused explicitly on English language development, and during the last block of the day, students were enrolled in elective courses like physical education, art, or Spanish.

Students' proficiency in Spanish, on the other hand, was valued only in instances in which it served utilitarian purposes (i.e., translating for other students or for teachers in relation to school). School-to-career students who spoke Spanish were rarely offered the opportunity to participate in classrooms for purposes other than translating. Students who had previously completed general education courses (e.g., American Literature) were utilized as a resource for helping students who were currently enrolled in those courses. The expectation that students serve as translators (without being compensated in a way equal to the service they provided to the school) exploited their linguistic skills and narrowed their biographies to the single dimension that could serve agents of the school.

Isabel's experience in an introductory Spanish class was illustrative of another way in which students' funds of knowledge were neglected. Having attended school regularly in El Salvador since the age of 7, her Spanish literacy skills were quite developed. She was, however, placed in a Spanish 1 course during the fourth block of the day, during which she "learned" introductory vocabulary—words and phrases that were most likely among her first words as a toddler—and simple grammatical structures. She explained, "Pues, hago lo mismo que los güeros, repito todo *(Well, I do the same as the white kids, I repeat everything)."* Her teacher had not questioned the appropriateness of her placement in this Spanish class—or at least had not achieved an alternative placement for her—providing her with the same course experience as the non-Spanish dominant learners in the class.

The Spanish program at WRHS privileged Castilian Spanish, which differed in important ways from Isabel's Salvadorian Spanish, so even when she should have had the opportunity to experience academic success, her Spanish knowledge and skills were dismissed. This placement in an introductory Spanish class completely disregarded her Spanish proficiency and biliteracy, and the absence of attempts to differentiate the curriculum to acknowledge her linguistic skills communicated that her Spanish was *less than* Castilian Spanish and sometimes even incorrect (Leeman, 2018). This missed opportunity to draw out and build on her linguistic skills in Spanish class was culturally insensitive and inequitable, and her placement in the introductory class simply filled space in her schedule. Moreover, the school's Spanish class for proficient speakers, which I had developed and taught when I was a teacher at the school, would have provided a more appropriate learning opportunity for her to further develop her Spanish literacy and to leverage her Spanish in developing academic literacies (Fránquiz & Salinas, 2011; García & Wei, 2014).

Another example of a missed opportunity to draw on students' background experiences in a meaningful way, an activity that was deployed with good intentions, was when Mrs. Durham asked students to explore the duality of their experiences of living in their home countries and in the United States. Sayra's illustrations of her "I Am From" poem hung in the hallway outside the classroom, along with the work of some her classmates. Three faces illustrated her poem: one face was covered with images of her experiences in the United States, one face was covered with images of her experiences in Mexico, and the middle face was constructed by one-half of each of the Mexico and United States faces (see image below). The face depicting her experiences in the United States showed relatively abstract happy images, like her school, trees, and a bright yellow sun. Her Mexico face was much more detailed, including images of people walking and talking together. The juxtaposition of her life in Mexico with her life in the United States is a powerful illustration of the multitude of rich experiences these students brought to the classroom.

Sayra's drawings representing her life in Mexico and in the United States were meaningful opportunities for reflection. However, the face in the middle in which her Mexico face and United States face were cut down the middle and joined to create a new face was a simplistic representation of how newcomers construct identities (Sarroub, 2002). The nuanced ways in which their experiences in their

80 • LEARNING TO HIDE

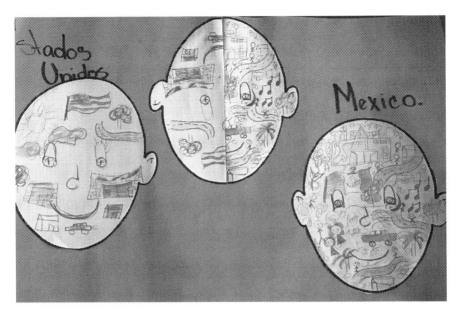

Sayra's Illustrated "I Am From" Poem.

home countries influence and transform their lives in the U.S. were lost through this crude mash-up of their identities.

Essentially, neglecting students' background experiences and knowledge devalued their life histories. Placing students into extant structures rather than transforming them demonstrated an impromptu response to their arrival and perpetuated the privileging of whiteness (i.e., regarding English as the dominant language and evading the complexity of identities). Even acknowledging that school funding is limited, there were institutional and pedagogical changes that could have communicated a more inclusive message.

Missed Opportunities to Integrate Newcomers into U.S. History

There were also missed opportunities to integrate newcomers into the national narrative of U.S. history and to disrupt the majoritarian stories that fill the textbooks used in high school history classes (Díaz & Deroo, 2020; Hilburn et al., 2016). Their textbook used simple language to make the content more accessible to the English Learners, but in doing so, it simplified history to a straightforward and unidimensional majoritarian story. While teachers can and should supplement and complicate monolithic curriculum, these opportunities were missed in this classroom.

In some instances, students seemed dumbfounded by the neglect of how the course material so obviously related to their lives. For example, as students were learning about immigration from Northern Europe during the mid-1800s, Mrs. Durham, sitting at her desk, referenced a chart from their textbook that depicted Ireland and Germany as the two main "sources of immigration" between 1820–1860. When Mrs. Sánchez finished translating it, Mrs. Durham asked, "So, who are immigrants?" There was laughter from all the students. She smiled and tilted her head, "I know we have a roomful..." and left her question hanging. Alejandro suggested, "Nosotros." She nodded and rephrased her question, asking, "Which two countries had the most immigrants?" Someone shouted, "Guatemala!" and they all laughed again because clearly, he was right. The room was full of Guatemalan immigrants. Mrs. Durham clarified with a roll of her eyes, "...in 1820?" and someone mumbled, "Ireland and England," and Mrs. Durham praised their answer.

The passage in the textbook most certainly resonated with the students in the room, especially the references to the pull factors of jobs and freedom and the push factors of violence and economic insecurity in their home countries that prompted immigration. However, the connections to current immigrants searching for jobs and an escape from the economic issues and violence in their home countries, especially for the students in this room, were completely neglected. The opportunity to explore current immigration in relation to the broader history of U.S. immigration and to validate their own reasons for im/migrating was lost as the immigrants of the mid-1800s were isolated in time. Furthermore, there was no discussion to problematize the romantic notions of immigration of Europeans as contrasted with the racialization and criminalization of immigrants arriving at Angel Island from Asian countries during the first half of the 20th century or of immigrants arriving in the late 1900s and early 2000s from Central American countries and Mexico (Rodríguez, 2015). The opportunity for critical connection across time and space was lost.

Another example of a missed opportunity to integrate newcomers into the narrative of U.S. history came when the students were learning about the Civil War era. The experience of Dred Scott, an enslaved man who had been taken from Missouri (in which slavery was allowed by law) to Illinois (in which slavery was outlawed) and then back to Missouri, served as fertile ground for an honest discussion of the United States' racist history. Scott and his wife, Harriet, who argued that they became free when they entered Illinois, sued for their freedom in Missouri. The Supreme Court's "Dred Scott decision" of 1857 ruled that enslaved persons were not citizens and thereby had no rights guaranteed to them (Scott v. Sandford, 1856). The way in which the status of "citizen" was equated with having "no rights" begged for discussion, especially in light of the many students who did not have legal status or who were in a liminal status as they waited for their immigration hearings. However, the students simply copied the statement into their notes and they quickly moved on to the next page of the textbook. Mrs. Durham ignored the blatantly racist Supreme Court decision and the legacy of such racism in the modern world.

82 • LEARNING TO HIDE

The brief passage included in the textbook about the Underground Railroad would have provided an important connection to students' lives as well.

> Other people worked together in secret to help slaves escape from the South. They let runaway slaves hide in their houses, barns, and basements. At night, the slaves would travel from one house to another. Eventually, they reached the North—and freedom. This way of escaping to freedom was called the Underground Railroad. (Duran et al., 2005, p. 134)

The students' experiences of school and community life mirrored the description in the passage and begged for connection, especially considering Mrs. Durham's earlier reference to her basement as a safe space for them following Trump's election. In addition, the passage would have served as an entry point into discussing "La Bestia," the train that runs northward through Mexico into the United States and which is named "the beast" because many migrants who ride atop it in the blistering sun are injured or killed on the harrowing journey. This comparison may have helped students conceptualize the danger and urgency of the enslaved persons seeking freedom and may have opened space for a discussion about modern-day slavery and indentured servitude.

One final example of missed opportunities to integrate students into the United States' historical narrative came when they learned about the women's suffrage movement that led to women earning the right to vote in 1920. Mrs. Durham concluded the passage matter-of-factly, stating, "Now in America, anyone over 18 can vote." As noted earlier, Mrs. Sánchez's translation offered an important caveat, adding, "as long as they are American citizens." Mrs. Durham's statement was an idealistic portrayal of the country, but completely left out the millions of citizens who do not have legal status that would afford them the right to vote. Mrs. Sánchez's quick addition to the translation clarified this, but there was still no discussion of the implications for the myriad ways people without legal status could participate as citizens.

The American historical narrative is long and complicated, and missing opportunities to integrate newcomers into this narrative is dismissive and ignorant of the learners in the room. Each missed opportunity taught the students that American history was a static story from the past and neglected to foster connections between the past, present, and future. In addition, the missed opportunities were instances of evading opportunities to confront the oppression that has constructed the inequities in the United States and also further perpetuated majoritarian stories of the historical narrative.

Missed Opportunities to Integrate Civic Education

Even though Mrs. Durham's class was a history class, there were missed opportunities to integrate civic education into the course. Beth Rubin (2012) asserts that U.S. history courses, required in schools across the country, are sites with great potential to integrate civics meaningfully into history. Increased attention to

Missed Opportunities in the Classroom and School • **83**

citizenship education is especially urgent for immigrants who arrive to the U.S. in adolescence, given the hurried nature of their schooling experience (i.e., accumulating graduation credits before they age out of the school system) (Banks, 2017; Jaffee, 2016).

In the ELL history classroom at WRHS, students learned symbolic gestures of American citizenship, like standing and reciting the Pledge of Allegiance each day, but with no discussion of the reasons behind Colin Kaepernick's decision to take a knee during the pregame national anthem (Reid, 2017). Amidst an enormously impactful historical moment, students grappled with learning to do life in America *and* to do life in America under Trump. Trump's election added to the stresses that students already experienced, as Caterín Michelle explained that she felt "at the same time nervous, fear, surprised..." when faced with living in the U.S. during a Trump presidency. They wondered if they would be deported and if their work permits would be removed or if their immigration cases would be disrupted. They questioned the politicization of their bodies in the U.S., asking, "Why doesn't Trump like Hispanics?" The historical moment was ripe for discussion of civil rights, civic participation, and collective strategies, especially in connection to previous and ongoing social justice movements.

Students, however, were strongly discouraged from participating in political dialogue. Mrs. Durham advised them with a serious tone as she introduced the short unit on elections in the two weeks leading up to the 2016 general election, "Politics are a taboo in society." She explained that discussion of politics can damage relationships and even asked students to explain back to her in writing the reasons that discussing politics was taboo. This was contradictory to what they had learned about the Bill of Rights earlier in the semester. The First Amendment, it seemed, guaranteed freedom of speech and expression *unless* the speech was political.

By discouraging political dialogue and action, Mrs. Durham disparaged the activism of people like Dolores Huerta and César Chávez, who fought for the rights of migrant farm workers during the 1960s, and she tacitly advised students to accept the status quo and remain hidden in the margins of society. The expectation seemed to be that students learn the rights guaranteed by the Bill of Rights in the U.S. Constitution but that they not exercise them. This dangerously implied that "We the People" was not inclusive of people like them. The tension, though, between teaching to amplify students' voices and acknowledging the reality of a political context that limits the rights of people who do not have legal status is real and one with which Mrs. Durham grappled; however, there are examples of justice-oriented citizenship education pedagogies (see, for example, Dabach et al., 2018).

Trump's promises to remove "bad hombres" carried implications for how newcomer students saw themselves. W. E. B. Du Bois (1903) reflected on how this "double-consciousness" positions Black and Indigenous people and People of Color in the world: "It is a peculiar sensation, this double-consciousness, this

84 • LEARNING TO HIDE

sense of always looking at one's self through the eyes of others, of measuring one's soul by the tape of a world that looks on in amused contempt and pity (p. 3). The racist alienation and nativist claims to the privileges of U.S.-born citizens most certainly prompted students to experience this "double-consciousness," positioning themselves as "Persons of Color" and sensing the implications of their bodies. The absence of any discussion of racism—even amidst the school's promised intolerance of "racist" comments—assumed a shared understanding of the experience. Understanding one's positionality and agency within a raced, classed society such as the U.S. requires critical analysis of the concept of racism and the forces that work to sustain and embolden it.

What students do not learn is just as notable as what they do learn. The missed opportunities are silences—loud silences—in the curriculum that evade essential questions of equity and justice. Citizenship requires active participation by all members, but students learned in this school and classroom that their citizenship was about self-preservation. This aim silenced them and encouraged acceptance of what *is* rather than fighting for what *ought to* or *could* be.

Missed Opportunities to Integrate Students into the School Community

The school as a whole segregated and distanced newcomer students and their families in a number of ways. The missed opportunities to integrate students into the school community pointed to the school's regard for newcomers as problems—with deficiencies in schooling and in English—and managed the problems by isolating them from the rest of the school. Newcomer students rarely left the hallway in which the ELL classrooms were located, and when they did, they seldom did so alone. As I noted earlier, non-ELL students rarely walked through the ELL hallway, and there was no interaction between them and ELL students when they did. This physical segregation from the rest of the school distanced students from the daily life of the school and physically relegated them to the margins, as their hallway was located in a corner of the school farthest from the main entrance.

The administration's decision to route attendance phone calls from Spanish-speaking families from the main office to Mrs. Durham's classroom distanced families from the office and administrative center of the school. The attendance clerk's refusal to continue to make and field phone calls from Spanish-speaking parents and caretakers was dismissive of an entire swath of the student population. Mrs. Durham's willingness to accept the phone calls in her classroom—a task that was then delegated to Mrs. Sánchez—was an attempt to serve Spanish-speaking families in the same way that English-dominant families were served. However, this added to the already long list of tasks Mrs. Durham and Mrs. Sánchez had taken on from the duties of the main office. In this way, newcomer students were out of sight and out of mind of the central office of the school.

Similarly, the school wide announcements broadcasted over the intercom each morning were solely in English, ignoring the student population who were non-

Missed Opportunities in the Classroom and School • **85**

English-dominant. Broadcasting announcements in Spanish would have communicated to the whole school community that Spanish was a part of their school and community. Although Mrs. Durham recognized the inequity in English-only announcements, she wearily admitted that most of the announcements (i.e., where to get parking passes or how to register for ACT-preparation courses) did not apply to newcomers anyway. This positioned Mrs. Durham as a gatekeeper to the information to which students had access. Diego's cheeky question, "¿Qué dijo *(What did he say?)*" after an especially lengthy series of announcements—and the ensuing laughter from the rest of the students—indicated that the students recognized that they were not the intended audience for the school wide announcements. Likewise, the rest of the school was allowed to ignore that a portion of the student body was marginal to or invisible in their own existence at school. They did not "hear them" or "see them," as the fundraiser tee shirts implored.

Another example that pointed to the marginalization of newcomer and ELL students was on the occasion of a visit to the school from the district's Representative in the U.S. House of Representatives. "All junior and senior" social studies classes were invited (i.e., required) to go to the school auditorium to hear him address the group. No ELL students attended because, as Mrs. Durham explained, "they wouldn't understand what he was saying anyway." ELL students could have benefitted from the experience of coming face-to-face with the Representative from their community who had a voice in Washington, DC, and English-dominant students would have benefitted from seeing ELLs in the same public space with them; moreover, keeping the ELL students out of the auditorium during this meeting allowed the U.S. Representative to ignore their presence as well. However, the additional logistical considerations of translating the monolingual Representative's remarks outweighed the perceived benefits to ELLs, the school, and the legislator.

Finally, the curious decision on the school's part to overlook a qualified bilingual applicant for the position of guidance counselor in the school—and instead chose to shift personnel so that the high school football coach could be placed in a teaching position at the high school—belied the school's purported commitment to serve all students well. Instead, they continued to rely on Mrs. Sánchez to enroll new students, evaluate transcripts, and register students for classes. Although Mrs. Sánchez was dedicated to helping students and their families navigate WRHS, ELLs and their families did not have access to the same professional guidance non-ELL students had. The disregard for the need to recruit and hire bilingual professionals—in addition to more bilingual paraeducators—revealed their evasion of opportunities to transform the school to serve its newcomer students and their families more equitably.

The missed opportunities to integrate newcomers into the larger school community thwarted experiences for newcomers and longstanding residents to interact in a public space and to claim belonging in that shared space. These missed opportunities perpetuated the idea that newcomers not cause a disruption in the status quo, essentially hiding them from the wider school community. This misrepresentation of a reality of a changing community evades opportunities to make sense of their new realities and plan for more equitable societal conditions for all people.

What I have called missed opportunities may actually discount the agency that social actors have in schools and classrooms. The school and teachers were not simply missing opportunities, they were evading them (Viesca & Gray, 2021). In doing so, they demonstrated a willful disregard for the possibilities for school to be a place that cultivates citizen identities motivated to act and to seek to understand, as well as to be a place for all young people to claim space and belonging, to see and be seen, and to hear and be heard, in the full public realm.

CHAPTER 7

THE PARADOXICAL TENSIONS OF SANCTUARY AND TRAP

I entered into this research with preexisting notions of citizenship that, even though framed by the construct of "cultural citizenship" (Rosaldo, 1994), were interpreted through my own lens of whiteness. Consistent with ethnographic study, I attended to the shared understandings for constructing, describing, and navigating the social world. The "epistemological humility" (Spradley, 1979) necessary in ethnographic work afforded me the opportunity to see through the students' experiences how "being different" (Rosaldo, 1994)—embodying a reality of Brownness—had very real implications for the public space in which to construct and exercise citizen identities. The quotidian relational, cultural, and social practices in this classroom and school narrowed newcomers' access to the public space in which they could see and be seen and hear and be heard—the students' t-shirts proclaiming a very sincere message to the school and beyond: "Hear us, see us."

A brief note is important here to acknowledge the unique context of constructing a citizen identity in a Brown body alongside the evolving presidential campaign of Donald Trump. It was happenstance that this study coincided with the 2016 general election in the United States. I was keenly aware in the weeks and days leading up to the election on November 8, 2016 that the polarized and vitriolic rhetoric surrounding the election was of historical import. Donald Trump's

Learning to Hide: The English Learning Classroom as Sanctuary and Trap
pages 87–99.
Copyright © 2024 by Information Age Publishing
www.infoagepub.com
All rights of reproduction in any form reserved.

bigoted and misogynistic assertions surfaced some of the most hateful factions of the underbelly of the U.S. social fabric and undermined the very idea of truth. This sociopolitical context offers a unique and important lens to understand how newcomers to the United States made sense of what I, as a lifelong American citizen, struggled to wrap my mind around.

Mrs. Durham's ELL classroom was a vibrant, busy space in which students found help and guidance with a wide range of needs and issues. They spent the vast majority of their school day in this and the other ELL classroom and in the hallway between them. They talked in multiple languages, learned and laughed together, and pulled pranks on one another and engaged in and resolved arguments; through these social experiences, they built a thriving community. The space served as a necessary sanctuary *from* the incessant demands of English and the feelings of otherness (Jaffe-Walter & Miranda, 2020), and also as a sanctuary *for* the development of hybrid identities (Irizarry, 2007; Sarroub, 2002) and to learn their rights and responsibilities as citizens of the United States (Banks, 2017).

However, the policies and practices surrounding language in WRHS isolated newcomer students from the general population of the school. Language policies and practices influence students' experiences of school in ways that transcend language. As Gitlin et al. (2003) assert,

> In subtle and complex ways, the school experience (in general, and specifically for students in ESL programs) not only helps produce margin and center, therefore making it possible to include and exclude various groups from some of the opportunities and benefits of residing at the center, but also 'places' immigrant students on the margins. (p. 117)

Placing and keeping newcomer students on the margins imposes real limits on the space in which they construct citizen identities. As such, the sanctuary of the ELL classroom was paradoxically a trap, and the policies and practices that placed them there served to justify and sustain it.

A closer look at the everyday sociocultural activities in the classroom elucidates the paradoxical tension of sanctuary and trap. As I made sense of my observations and interviews with social actors in the classroom, I learned that what I understood as citizenship was unrecognizable to me in this space. Instead, considering citizenship practices as situated within the routine of everyday life, I began to understand the relational, emotional, and cultural expressions of citizenship within this classroom and the conditions and context in which students constructed citizen identities. In addition, I began to question the school's commitment to integrating newcomers into the school and by extension into the community; in acts both subtle and overt, I observed how newcomer students' experiences of school lacked aspirational guidance and instead focused on meeting newcomers' immediate survival needs. WRHS became a context in which newcomers' marginalized positions narrowed their biographies and their aspirations for their futures.

LEARNING IN THE MARGINS

Human beings are always learning in the course of daily life, and, in addition to the content knowledge and skills schools aim to teach, students also learn about who they and others are and how they are positioned in society through their experiences of school. The mismatch between newcomers' realities and school, the different aims for citizenship implied by different kinds of care, and the missed opportunities to integrate newcomers into the curriculum and life of the school illuminated the experiences of newcomers in Washington River High School and spotlighted the growing pains the school experienced as it attempted to respond to its new students. So, what did newcomer students learn in the margins of Washington River High School?

Learning from Mismatch

The newcomer students at WRHS experienced a mismatch between their realities and the extant policies and practices at school (Deschenes et al., 2001). The mismatches, revealed in the quotidian life of the school and classroom, were instructive in shaping understandings within the complex space we all negotiate between Self and Other (Biesta, 2004). What did newcomer and longstanding resident students learn from these mismatches as they constructed citizen identities?

It was clear that WRHS structures, policies, and practices were resistant to adapt to newcomer students' dual realities, brought into sharp focus after the election of Donald Trump on November 8, 2016. Trump's "America First" agenda and anti-immigrant rhetoric affected students by adding another kind of stress to their life experiences. Newcomers were the "problem" of very few staff members at the school; at WRHS, only a small fraction of the staff was involved in meeting the needs of newcomers, including providing instruction to them. This required Mrs. Durham, Mrs. Sánchez, and the other ELL teachers to shoulder the responsibility for all newcomers and allowed everyone else to ignore them.

It is no wonder that Mrs. Durham and Mrs. Sánchez felt so protective and responsible for meeting students' needs, and so exhausted from the work. Furthermore, since the school regarded newcomers as a problem (as evidenced in their deficit-based placements in the ELL program), Mrs. Durham's willingness to "contain" them was an easy out for the rest of the staff. Other faculty and staff members evaded the responsibility to integrate newcomers, and teachers relied on Mrs. Durham (which also meant Mrs. Sánchez) to communicate test dates and other class information. As such, the newcomer students were regarded as "Mrs. Durham's students" instead of "our students."

Next, even though the school as a whole was dismissive and neglectful of its responsibility to meet newcomers' needs, leaving the work to the teachers and staff in the ELL program, newcomers and their families looked to the school to meet the numerous and varying needs they had as they transitioned to a new country and community. Newcomers arrived with a range of needs as they transitioned to their new country and community. They managed immigration cases, enrolled children (or themselves) in school (with all the accompanying requirements that entails), secured housing and work and found transportation, including obtaining insurance and registration for vehicles. In cases in which they did not have documentation to secure the necessary requirements (e.g., not having documentation to obtain a driver's license), they risked encounters with authorities and additional fines for infractions. In the New Latinx Diaspora context of Washington River, school was the place where the bulk of newcomers' needs were addressed.

These services were subsumed into the work of the school, and thus, reconstructed the purposes of school. Acknowledging the important role of school as a public space, I question the notion that school—or more accurately, two to three individuals within the school—ought to take on the bulk of the responsibility for serving the full range of newcomers' needs in NLD communities. Schools that are aimed at educating students equitably simply cannot be faced with the choice of helping students and their families meet their survival needs or leaving them to flounder on their own.

Through the practice of English as the sole language of instruction students learned that English was privileged in the school and was the language of learning (i.e., learning English preceded learning subject matter). This practice disregarded and devalued the multilingualism and literacies newcomer students embodied (Fránquiz & Salinas, 2011; García & Wei, 2014). Even with the translations that Mrs. Sánchez provided, the students wrote notes and took quizzes and tests in English; there were far fewer opportunities for students to think about content in their dominant languages. Furthermore, by perpetuating the status quo of English-only instruction, the school participated in a larger project of tacitly evading more equitable learning experiences in which students could learn through multiple languages.

Another troublesome result of the dominance of English in the everyday practices of the school (e.g., school announcements) was that newcomer students learned that their proficiencies in languages other than English did not afford them full access to the school community. They learned that the announcements—and all the events and special notices they communicated—were not intended for them. More problematic still is that they learned that English-speaking students *were* the intended audience; English afforded full participation and belonging in the school community, and by extension, the nation-state (Russell & Mantilla-Blanco, 2022).

The mismatches between the policies and practices of WRHS and newcomers' realities revealed the disequilibrium that schools in new receiving communities in the NLD experience. The demographic change in their schools and communities tilted their world. It would be simplistic to blame the mismatch on the durable institution of schooling because institutions are not static structures. *People* make up institutions, and it is through their actions (intentional or not) that institutions are transformed (Soo Hoo, 2004). Institutions are not unchangeable, but it takes political will to act in service of change; efforts to integrate newcomer students were noticeably absent—or at best, makeshift—throughout WRHS. The absence of the political will to transform in response to newcomers taught all members of the school community to uncritically sustain the project of evading equitable education and inclusion and sent strong implicit messages about who belonged.

Learning from Different Kinds of Care

Different people in this classroom—the teacher, the paraeducator, and the students—manifested care in different ways, which implied different aims of schooling for newcomer students and different understandings of citizenship. Care became about saving one another from people and consequences with institutionalized power, perpetuating the dominance of English, and amplifying majoritarian stories of whiteness. What did newcomer students learn from the different kinds of care as they constructed citizen identities?

Mrs. Durham's care was oriented toward survival and protection, certainly important aims. However, these students in their young lives had already demonstrated their capability to survive. While their journeys to Washington River were as diverse as they were, they had learned to navigate and negotiate the terrain of relationships and complex systems to arrive in this space. When they could go to Mrs. Durham for solving problems that did not relate to school, they learned to seek out and rely on people with institutionalized power to take care of them. Similarly, they learned that manipulating people was necessary to gain access to services that could help them succeed in school.

But Mrs. Durham also made students feel cared for and valued. She earned their trust, treated that trust very seriously, and had a reputation for being supportive of newcomers and a fierce advocate for the "family" that was the ELL program (past and present members included). That kind of care is not nothing. Students learned from this care that there were people who worked for them and with them to create good lives for themselves, even as they were bombarded with negative exclusionary messages about immigrants. They learned that they were not alone in the world—that they had a role in creating and sustaining networks and communities of care. They learned that there were safe sanctuary spaces and there was solidarity within them. Those are all deeply important lessons in the construction of a citizen identity.

Mrs. Sánchez's care cultivated in students a sense of belonging. Through her culturally mediated care, she modeled and communicated to students the experience of claiming physical and cultural space and belonging in a space not inclusive of them (Gray, 2021). The intersecting dimensions of her multicultural, multilingual identity and life experiences undergirded her high expectations for students and culturally relevant care (Watson et al., 2016). Students learned that a young Latina woman *belonged* in the school and ought to be regarded as someone with institutional power. As Mrs. Sánchez's presence attested, cultural representation matters in schooling with the aim of fostering belonging for all students (see, for example, Graham, 1987; Milner, 2006).

92 • LEARNING TO HIDE

Relatedly, Mrs. Sánchez modeled a critique of the stratification of society. Having experienced marginalization herself, she named inequities and injustices in the social life of the United States; in doing so, she validated many of the students' experiences. Through this validation, students learned that there were others who were incensed by injustice. They learned how they could critique the endemic systemic racism in the United States, and they learned *that they could* critique injustices.

Mrs. Sánchez's bilingualism facilitated students' understanding and construction of a multicultural and multilingual identity. That is, she did not just translate *words*, she also translated *worlds* (Freire, 1970)—the norms, values, and routines of the diverse cultures in the classroom because she was able to function within and between cultures in this multicultural context. Students saw themselves in her multicultural, multilingual self, and they learned to recognize and value their identities and experiences. However, because language constructs reality (Boroditsky, 2011), they also learned through Mrs. Sánchez's interchangeable use of "American" and "white" that Americans were white. This seemingly simple discursive practice conveyed subtle messages about race and belonging, complicating her modeling of belonging.

Finally, the ways in which students demonstrated care taught important lessons, too. As they mapped and taught one another to navigate the underground and margins of school life—and by extension, community life—they learned to move quietly and unnoticed from safe space to safe space to accomplish what they needed to do. They may have claimed space in the margins, but they stayed on the margins. As such, they learned a problematic location of citizenship.

Overwhelmingly, though, students learned to take care of one another—that their own belonging was wrapped up with their peers' belonging. Sayra's description of the social dynamics of spatial claims in the cafeteria offered a lesson about sticking together and including one another, especially when they experienced a space as contested between the "Hispanics" and *las gringas*. It was important to reach out and invite other "Hispanics" to the table when exclusion from *las gringas'* table was presumed. As such, students learned that there was strength in numbers.

Students also learned to support one another through sharing and supporting one another. While there were underlying sentiments of competition or comparison, the culture was mainly one of collaboration and cooperation. Competition manifested in relation to linguistic differences, such as when Caterín Michelle noted that Alejandro was the most intelligent in the class because he spoke English well, or when one student received more praise than another for their work. However, even when the competitive spirit emerged, the spirit of cooperation and support overcame it. Students learned that while they all had different strengths and that they could depend on their peers to use their strengths to help each other.

The cultural notions of *respeto* and *educación* influenced how students cared for each other as well. Drawing on their "familial capital" (Yosso, 2005), students learned that they would be held accountable for behaviors like courtesy, helpfulness, and maturity in this classroom, not only by the official authorities but also by one another. Because of the familial nature of the culture of the classroom, students expected each other to be respectful. Even though accountability is often related to following the rules, the cultural values embedded in *respeto* and *educación* had more to do with how they treated each other (Valdés, 1996).

Students, in their roles as guides to students new to the school and program and in taking care of the classroom, learned stewardship as well. They learned that they had an important role in welcoming new students and helping them feel at home as they showed them the ropes through the hallways and cafeteria, and even in the classroom. They also learned to be stewards, taking care of the physical space of the classroom.

While Mrs. Durham worked tirelessly to meet students' needs, she did so necessarily with a mostly deficit-based perspective about newcomers (i.e., focusing on what they needed). Mrs. Sánchez offered a more critical perspective of the students' experiences (and her own) in the United States, and she worked toward more aspirational aims of belonging and claiming rights. The students supported each other by carving out space in the underground of the school and guiding each other through it. All these kinds of care fostered learning that influenced the construction of citizen identities, but *what* students learned varied widely and implied different conceptions of citizenship.

Learning from Missed Opportunities

Even with the best of intentions, there were missed opportunities to connect school to students' lives and to integrate students into the school and community in meaningful and justice-oriented ways. There were also missed opportunities to cultivate critical democratic citizenship practices and foster belonging in the wider school and community. Not only were these missed opportunities for academic and social learning, but they also were instructive in teaching newcomers who and what mattered in school and in society. What did students learn from these missed opportunities?

There were a number of missed opportunities to draw out and leverage students' funds of knowledge. The students in the classroom had life experiences, knowledge, and skills upon which new knowledge could be constructed, but these were neglected as they were placed into the ELL program based on their deficiency in English. Instruction in English, with some supplemental translation and interpretation, meant that students learned that English was the language of learning. Conversely, students learned that their life experiences, knowledge, and skills did not have academic value in this space. Even Isabel's knowledge of and literacy in Spanish was dismissed through her placement in an introductory Spanish class. Even though they were encouraged to share their experiences and were not discouraged from speaking languages other than English with each other, these missed opportunities thwarted opportunities to build on and enrich what they already knew (García & Wei, 2014).

94 • LEARNING TO HIDE

The students' placement in the ELL program made it clear that they were different, and the physical placement of the ELL classrooms on the periphery of the school imposed marginality. Students learned through their segregation, quite clearly, that their place was in the margins of the school. Moreover, the rarity of the occasions on which they left the ELL classroom hallway reinforced their marginal existence. The missed opportunity to integrate students more fully and authentically into the school community taught them to assimilate into the extant structures of the school.

There were multiple missed opportunities to connect newcomer students to the U.S. history curriculum and to integrate them into the narrative of United States history. Students learned instead that their presence in the United States was unrelated to earlier immigrants and migrants and irrelevant to the American story. Students learned a majoritarian story of immigration that applauded the perseverance of European immigrants who, while called immigrants, were not like them.

Students also learned, through the uncritical discussions about Donald Trump and the potential consequences of his proposed policies, that their bodies were racialized and criminalized in the United States. They learned that a huge swath of the country, especially in Nebraska, had supported Trump, cultivating a sense of paranoia about the tenuous nature of their claims to rights and belonging in the country in which they lived. Perhaps most dangerous was that they learned that exercising their right to speak their truth was "taboo in society."

What students did not learn in their history class is perhaps of even greater import. Students learned an incomplete narrative that did not account for the long history of the criminalization of immigrants that resulted in limits on their civil and human rights. The missed opportunities to integrate civic education into the daily classroom and school practices and curriculum perpetuated the status quo and reduced citizenship to symbolic and shallow rituals. Especially notable in a historical moment of such tremendous import, students did not learn the full range of their rights and responsibilities as human beings, as small-c citizens, in the United States.

These missed opportunities were neglected opportunities in which teachers and other school staff evaded their responsibility to work with newcomer students and address equity. The persistence of the status quo—and a general resistance to change—manifested the maintenance of a culture of whiteness (including the privileging of English) at WRHS and in Washington River in general. The school changed their daily operations very little, if at all, in response to its newcomer students.

An Emergent Citizen Identity

Taken together, it is clear that there is much work to be done for schools to transform to provide newcomer students an equitable opportunity to construct citizen identities within the full realm of the public space. The resistance to change in this NLD community and in the public high school that serves its residents

The Paradoxical Tensions of Sanctuary and Trap • 95

is revealed against the backdrop of the descriptions of daily life of newcomers within the school. Overall, WRHS was resistant to change as evidenced in the persistent mismatches for newcomer students, relegating them to the margins of the school. This location of citizenship construction negates opportunities for newcomers to experience the full realm of public space and to enter into the public consciousness. Furthermore, it evades opportunities for interaction and understanding across and through difference.

An image of a citizen identity emerges by looking closely at what students learned through the mismatches, different kinds of care, and missed opportunities in Washington River High School. The multidimensional citizen identity that emerges is complex and paradoxical. They are at once dependent upon others and agentive. They at once understand themselves as a problem and as a community. They are at once connected to their cultures and languages and deculturalized. They experience both belonging and exclusion. They at once care for one another and fend for themselves. They at once learn to claim space and to remain in the margins. They at once question the world and accept it. They at once learn to insist, "Hear us, see us" and to hide.

This emergent citizen identity prompts the questions: What kind of citizen do we need? Toward what aim ought we to orient schooling for immigrant students, especially those who arrive as high school-aged students? A return to the earlier description of the sociopolitical context of the United States is worthwhile in answering this question. We are politically and socially polarized, and this polarization was exacerbated by Trump's election to the presidency and his administration's harmful policies; three years into a Biden administration shows very little difference. We cling to sameness, even as we become more diverse, and refuse to dialogue across differences. Similarly, the notion of *truth* is driven by alignment to like ideologies, and truth claims are evaluated and spread or suppressed by their fidelity to biases. The ideological orientation of neoliberalism cultivates competition, and the mythology of the rugged individual veils the racist foundations of the country and ignores the persistent resultant wealth disparities across racial lines. Given this contentious context, what kind of citizen do we need right now?

If the current context can offer a vision of the citizens we *have*, and if we can agree that what we have is not working (i.e., everyone is *not* regarded as equal), we can leverage the current context to construct a vision of a "more perfect Union" and the citizens who can work toward that vision. The country will need to heal from the enormous damage done to human and civil rights throughout the Trump presidency (i.e., unlawful separation of immigrant and refugee families, hyper-criminalization of immigrants, increased militarization of the police, rampant and unapologetic misogyny, vitriolic polarization, and on and on) and the enduring work of a conservative Trump-appointed majority of the U.S. Supreme Court (Liptak, 2023). However, there is also healing necessary for the people who, even before they elected Trump to the presidency, were enraged at a country in which they did not feel seen or heard (Wuthrow, 2018).

96 • LEARNING TO HIDE

This healing will require citizens who have a deep sense of justice, a sense of justice that acknowledges the harmful legacies that privilege some and oppress others (Ladson-Billings, 2004). In addition, citizens will need to have deep knowledge of the rights and responsibilities guaranteed to all people in the U.S. Constitution (Banks, 2017). This includes an orientation toward justice that may mean sacrificing one's privilege to disrupt structures, policies, and practices that oppress others (Allen, 2004).

Given the political polarization in the United States and the vitriol sustaining it, we need citizens who can see and hear across difference, even if it means bearing witness to anger and resentment. Moreover, we need citizens who *seek* difference as we redefine "civil discourse" to recognize and leverage the power of conflict and deliberation to enhance understanding (Hess, 2008). An important part of learning to listen to each other will be to establish a shared understanding of truth, even as we acknowledge multiple realities. This must include repairing trust in our fellow citizens.

Finally, as we seek difference, we need citizens with the will to act in service of the common good. An explicit aim of critical democratic citizenship addresses the cultivation of citizenship practices that allow all people to claim rights and experience belonging—to be equal—in the United States (Abu El-Haj, 2009; Flores, 2003). Especially relevant to life for newcomers in the U.S., citizenship must be understood, as Flores (2003) asserts, "an active process of claiming rights rather than the passive acquisition of an arbitrary and limited set of rights" (p. 295). This must include an acceptance of others' claims to rights and belonging in spaces where they have been historically excluded or marginalized.

The challenges facing schools in NLD receiving communities are many, but the diversity that is so essential to democracy is enriched by the arrival of newcomers in these contexts. Newcomers and longstanding resident students must have deliberately cultivated opportunities for interaction and dialogue (e.g., offering bilingual social studies classes) to regard one another in what Danielle Allen (2004) calls "political friendship." If this is to happen, schools must transform in response to newcomers rather than justify segregated arrangements based solely on newcomers' deficits in English.

If, as bell hooks (1994) insisted, the classroom is a space with transformative potential, we have to believe that social change can happen through education as the practice of critical democratic citizenship. However, too often this belief is diminished to a slogan touted in diversity and inclusion statements. In places like Washington River High School, statements of "nondiscrimination" and stated commitments to educate "all students" evade opportunities to address equity through the daily practice of school.

EVASION PEDAGOGIES IN
WASHINGTON RIVER HIGH SCHOOL

Resistance to change in NLD receiving communities is normal and expected; change is hard. However, it must not be tolerated long term. Communities can only claim to be "New" Latinx Diaspora contexts for so long. Given that Latinx immigrants and migrants have been arriving and settling in Washington River since the 1990s, there are some promising signs, although few, at WRHS that demonstrate small changes can make a big difference. There are also a number of signs that the school is neglecting to serve newcomers well, and at the same time, refusing to be transformed by them.

Various social actors in WRHS, by evading opportunities "to address equity through the project of teaching and learning," enacted what Kara Viesca and I (2021) have termed "evasion pedagogies." Drawing on Annamma et al.'s (2017) conceptualization of color-evasiveness, which acknowledges the active role in evading color beyond just being "blind" to color, we extend color-evasiveness to describe "evasion pedagogies." Evasion pedagogies serve

> to evade solving the fundamental problem of inequity in our schools and society through the project of teaching and learning. Thus, evasion pedagogies serve to sustain the status quo and are powerful tools to maintain oppressive projects like white supremacy, heteronormativity, gender binaries, patriarchy, ableism and classism, often under the cover of the institution of schooling. (Viesca & Gray, 2021, p. 1)

In evasion pedagogies, various social actors perform cultural "scripts" (Gutiérrez et al., 1995) of teaching and learning, most often performing teaching as surveillance and learning as compliance. In the daily performances of these scripts, pedagogy is constructed—just like citizen identities. The scripts undergirding teaching and learning are revealed through the lens of evasion pedagogies. Below, I offer a handful of examples that were promising signs of change in the school and describe the scripts that undergird these quotidian practices and policies; then, I turn to the more ubiquitous signs of scripts that constructed evasion pedagogies at WRHS.

Promising Signs of Change

There were signs at WRHS that small changes made a difference in newcomers' experiences of school. Clearly, Mrs. Sánchez's presence in the classroom was a promising sign that the school acknowledged their obligation to communicate with non-English dominant students and families (Ernst-Slavit & Wenger, 2006). The addition of two other bilingual paraeducators gave access to the help and guidance newcomers needed as they learned to navigate their new school. WRHS also scheduled interpreters to be on call at parent-teacher conferences so that teachers could communicate with parents and caretakers who were monolingual Spanish speakers; this was an improvement from just a few years earlier when

LEARNING TO HIDE

the school improvised communication by having students translate between the parents and teachers at conferences. Even the routing of attendance phone calls to Mrs. Sánchez demonstrated an attempt on the school's part to facilitate communication between school and Spanish-speaking students and families—although this separate line distanced them from the main office. The script undergirding these efforts conveyed the school's acknowledgement of their changing demographics but stopped short of a real reckoning with how all demographics might be more deliberately represented throughout the school.

It was also encouraging to see ELL students integrated into classrooms with the rest of the school for the 20-minute homeroom time four days a week. General education students and ELL students had opportunities to interact in these environments, even if they could not communicate fully through spoken language. I also noted that more ELL and newcomer students—although still a very small number—had begun to participate in extracurricular athletics activities at the school. Again, these activities were informal opportunities for students of all backgrounds to interact. These intercultural interactions were guided by scripts of hesitant encounters between longstanding residents and newcomers as they engaged in parallel activity, even if they did not establish enduring relationships.

Unfortunately, the promising signs of change at WRHS were much more improvised than intentional. As such, the intercultural encounters remained mostly incidental and without deliberate integration of cultures. Furthermore, there was no intentional creation of spaces in which longstanding residents might feel a structural shift (i.e., changing the lunch menus, sharing the announcements in more than one language, etc.); as such, newcomers were expected to assimilate into the extant spaces in the school.

Evasion Pedagogies at Play

Numerous manifestations of evasion pedagogies reveal scripts for assimilation and conformity to dominant ways of being at WRHS. The clearest sign that WRHS refused to be transformed by its newcomer students was the absence of any school wide inclusion of Spanish-language announcements or assemblies. The school was not meeting the newcomer students in the middle and conveyed the expectation that newcomers ought to assimilate to the established culture of the school and community. The languages of newcomers were viewed as a problem instead of a resource, and the most striking result of this disregard was the segregation and isolation of newcomer students in the ELL hallway. Thus, scripts of the dominance of English were at play.

While WRHS hired bilingual paraeducators, the school passed over a bilingual applicant for the guidance counselor position and did not actively recruit or hire bilingual teachers. This demonstrated that the school was not committed to fostering change in the teaching demographics so that they might more closely mirror those of their students. There was really no change at all in the general operation of the school, including hiring decisions, in response to newcomers. Newcomers were also asked to blend in; they were encouraged to follow the crowd and to learn to be a part of the school as it existed. The script of assimilation, again, communicated to them that they were the ones who were expected to change.

The Spanish classes were disappointingly ignorant of who was in them and privileged Castilian Spanish. This was both dismissive of Spanish-proficient students' knowledge and experiences and neglectful of the opportunity to foster bilingualism that could facilitate relationships and interactions among actual residents of Washington River rather than preparing them for tours of Spain. As I often reminded my own high school Spanish learners, monolingualism is curable; taking classes in high school to learn Spanish was one way to cure it but neglecting Central American and Mexican dialects of Spanish was exclusionary and dismissive of the Spanish spoken right in Washington River. This communicated a message of disregard for the knowledge and experiences of newcomers and privileged bilingualism only when English came first.

Finally, the multitude of missed opportunities to integrate newcomers into the narrative of United States history, to cultivate a strong civic education for newcomers, and to integrate newcomers into the life and learning of the school and community communicated a message of temporariness at best and exclusion at worst. Newcomers learned through the school's improvised attempts to serve them equitably that they were merely tolerated and that the mismatches between them and school created a burden for the school. Perhaps even more problematic in terms of evasion pedagogies were the missed opportunities to make newcomers seen and heard by longstanding residents; pedagogy is political, even if it is constructed by the absence of action (Nieto, 2006).

Students and some faculty and staff members constructed counterscripts as well (Gutiérrez et al., 1995). Students shrewdly navigated the margins they inhabited at the school, and the school increased bilingual communication efforts. Monolingual teachers made efforts to accommodate newcomers' language needs, and newcomer students supported each other by sharing information and work. These agentive acts were important steps in prompting change, but within the fossilized ideological assumptions undergirding the life of the school and community, they were not enough.

While Mrs. Durham's ELL classroom at Washington River High School was a sanctuary where newcomer students experienced belonging, support, and inclusion, it was also a trap held fast by evasion pedagogies. School is a space where students construct citizen identities. As such, contexts like WRHS—in which students of diverse backgrounds and experiences come together—must be sites where students learn and practice civic knowledge (e.g., civil and human rights) and skills (e.g., dialogue and deliberation) as they learn alongside each other and learn to live together. *All* students must see themselves in the U.S. Constitution's promise to protect the "inalienable rights" of "We the People" so that they might be the citizens we need.

CHAPTER 8

"HEAR US, SEE US"

The context of Washington River offers insight into the growing pains associated with demographic change in an NLD receiving community and school. It also offers useful lessons for moving forward toward more equitable and productive schooling practices for schools welcoming newcomers. As students in Mrs. Durham's classroom listened to the instructions for selling t-shirts to fund a field trip to the zoo, the message on the shirts was an ironic nod to their experiences in the school and community. "Hear Us, See Us," the shirt implored. The conditions that necessitated sanctuary and created and sustained the trap in the ELL classroom were instructive in understanding the evasion pedagogies at play in the classroom and school. What might it mean to hear and see newcomer students? Further, what might it look like to deliberately foster democratic citizenship practices that cultivate belonging for all students?

Disrupting evasion pedagogies requires, above all else, noticing—seeing and hearing—each other, but paying particular attention to those who have been historically minoritized and marginalized (Allen, 2004). Through noticing, we can begin to understand each other's realities and elevate and amplify the voices that have been oppressed. When we embody a stance of "epistemological humility" (Spradley, 1979), we think and act through inquiry. Disrupting evasion pedagogies also requires that we regard one another as agentive in the spaces we construct and navigate, and that we understand that actualizing our own humanity

---

Learning to Hide: The English Learning Classroom as Sanctuary and Trap
pages 101–107.
Copyright © 2024 by Information Age Publishing
www.infoagepub.com
All rights of reproduction in any form reserved.

102 • LEARNING TO HIDE

requires that we advocate for and insist upon the self-actualization of others (Viesca & Gray, 2021).

A long line of critical scholars, especially Black and Indigenous scholars and scholars of color have shown us how to do this (e.g., García & Wei, 2014; Gay, 2002; Kimmerer, 2013; Ladson-Billings & Tate, 1995; Lomawaima & McCarty, 2002; Paris & Alim, 2017; Simpson, 2017). They have all asked us to *notice* and learn from students who have been relegated to the margins. Disrupting evasion pedagogies and enacting humanizing pedagogies requires attention to multiple dimensions of the education system. First, we have to deconstruct what we mean by "school" and reconstruct a system that more equitably serves all students. Second, we have to orient ourselves toward equity by recognizing and disrupting oppressive ideologies and ways of thinking. And third, we must walk intentionally toward equity. Using Washington River High School as a frame of reference, I offer examples of how these steps might look.

Deconstructing School: Disrupting the System

Communities like Washington River do not just change overnight. The work of schools is influenced by the systems that construct and sustain the life and economy of the community. The corporations that recruit and hire immigrant and migrant workers—even those without authorization to work—need to shoulder some of the work of integrating newcomers into their new lives and communities (e.g., Lamphere, 1992; Lamphere et al., 1994; Stull, Broadway, & Erickson, 1992). Corporations that continue to profit from low-paid workers must be forced to reckon with and bear the weight of the work it takes to make a life in a new place, including paying workers a living wage. Mrs. Durham's and Mrs. Sánchez's work to ensure that their students were being paid fairly for the hours they worked and to monitor the number of hours the newcomer minors worked was admirable, but it was unfair to burden them with this work. Schools cannot be tasked with holding corporations to an ethic of responsibility; this needs to be the responsibility of the public.

Community organizations can also take a more intentional role in welcoming newcomers to their communities. Efforts by community organizations like the Kiwanis Club in Washington River—which provided transportation (bicycles) to fifteen students—or the Children's Fund—which granted funding for eyeglasses or dental care—were helpful. However, as Mrs. Durham acknowledged, their funds were not infinite. The participation of other community and civic organizations in meeting newcomers' needs—perhaps in cooperation with the schools—would alleviate some of the work newcomers must do to transition to their new community (Levine, 2007; Putnam, 2000).

Representation matters in demographically changing communities, and the administration, faculty, staff, and governing bodies influencing the work of the schools must be reflective of the demographics they serve. In Washington River, not one member of the district's Board of Education was a Latinx person, and the district administrators were all white and almost entirely men. This demographic mismatch in decision-making spaces must be rectified if we are serious about equity and inclusion.

It could be argued that WRHS professionals were not reflective of their demographics because there were no teachers with Latinx or immigrant identities seeking jobs there. While that may be the case, there must be a systematic effort to recruit and hire bilingual teachers and administrators and other staff who can communicate with non-English dominant students and their families. Newcomers need to be able to communicate with the school's office personnel to report absences and to be notified of students' absences; they also need to be able to communicate with the guidance counselors to discuss class registration and mental health concerns. Bilingual staff members would also be helpful in facilitating communication between the nurse and new students and their families to inform them of the required immunizations and documentation needed and to support their students' health. As Mrs. Durham admitted, the school "should do a lot more in both languages." All students should have access to all the information that is disseminated to the students in the school, and they ought to be able to participate meaningfully in the life of the school—outside of the ELL classroom and hallway.

There are also systemic implications for representation in educator preparation. Teacher education models that promote, recruit, and support bilingual teachers will be a crucial support to schools with multilingual student populations; a critical pedagogy component of these programs will develop teachers who acknowledge the political nature of their work and can help students learn critical practices of democratic citizenship (Abu El-Haj, 2009). Similarly, schools need to be supportive of alternative teacher education pathways like teacher residencies that cultivate learning to teach within a specific context and "grow-your-own" programs that work to help paraeducators obtain teacher licensure (Bickmore et al., 2005; Gatti, 2016; Grossman et al., 2009; Grossman & Loeb, 2008; Hammerness & Matsko, 2012). Furthermore, these alternate pathways may need financial support from the private foundations that supplement school district funding through fundraising efforts. There will always be a long wish list for what schools need but privileging the recruitment and retention of bi/multilingual, multicultural teachers would speak volumes about the district's priorities.

Teacher preparation programs could require proficiency in at least one other language to foster a cultural shift toward multilingualism; these programs should also include courses in which teacher candidates learn language acquisition strategies and strategies for working with English learners (Hamann & Reeves, 2013). If teachers' efforts to become multilingual are to be validated and encouraged, education funding must support their efforts through scholarships, grants, and loan forgiveness to learn a community language (e.g., through immersive summer experiences in language schools, community experiences, and/or internships). While preservice teachers largely shoulder the cost of international and multilingual experiences through study abroad programs, financially supporting this work

104 • LEARNING TO HIDE

would convey the public's commitment to integrating multilingual citizens into the social fabric of the United States.

Experiences to cultivate cultural proficiency and attention to multicultural education and critical pedagogy in all educator preparation courses will be especially important in developing teachers who empathize with and support newcomers while confronting inequities and disrupting the status quo of ideologically undergirded institutions (Bartolomé, 2004; Chou & Tozer, 2008; Conklin, 2008). Finally, bilingual paraeducators must also be compensated more appropriately for the work they do. Mrs. Sánchez earned less than $12 per hour as a paraeducator and clocked separate hours for interpretation and translation work at a slightly higher rate; ironically, her work in the ELL classroom was largely interpretation and translation, but she was not compensated for it in that space. Additional training and development opportunities will provide paraeducators with the tools they need to purposefully assist students in their school experiences as well (Ernst-Slavit & Wenger, 2006).

At the systemic level, there are also implications for educational leadership and policy. For example, it is important to acknowledge that many newcomers arrive in the United States with limited formal schooling and/or gaps in their schooling experiences. Newcomers at WRHS carried a burden of worry about earning enough credits in English-only classes to graduate before they aged out of the system. Alternate pathways to graduation for these students would offer a remedy to the "race" students enter when they arrive in U.S. schools; these pathways, however, must include language support and careful attention to the background experiences of newcomers.

There are a range of ways in which we can work to disrupt evasion pedagogies at the systemic level. Insisting on an ethic of corporate responsibility acknowledges that the life of the community is co-constructed. Attention to who has a seat at the table where decisions are being made demonstrates a commitment to inclusion. Furthermore, educator preparation has an obligation to foster critical consciousness to embody teaching as a political act that is oriented toward equity and justice.

Orienting Ourselves Toward Equity: Disrupting Oppressive Ideologies

Ideologies undergird the everyday work of schools and educators, and when they are invisible, they foment misunderstandings and cultural exclusion. Disrupting evasion pedagogies requires interrogating oppressive ideologies, especially those that are universal in hyper-conservative contexts like Washington River (i.e., whiteness, nativism, English-only). Whiteness is a durable and fossilized ideology that privileges an ethic of hard work and rugged individualism with no regard for the structural challenges imposed by racialization and inherited wealth disparities (Spring, 2012). The ideology of whiteness constructs and advances ideas like the so-called "achievement gap" to justify unequal outcomes among different groups of students, and it perpetuates the myth of meritocracy—the idea that if we just work hard enough, we will be successful (Sensoy & DiAngelo,

2017). These harmful ideas embedded in whiteness place blame on students and their families for the mismatches they encounter at school and the socioeconomic legacy of generational poverty.

Nativism is an ideology embedded in whiteness, and it constructs ideas about who belongs and is regarded with human and civil rights within national borders. Nativism is to blame for the racialization and gradual criminalization of immigrants and migrants, especially those from Mexico and the Central American countries of Guatemala, El Salvador, and Honduras (Santa Ana, 2002). A more honest acknowledgement of the ways that the United States has constructed immigration as a problem, and indeed, been complicit in destabilizing Central American and Mexican governments and economies is necessary for disrupting this oppressive ideology.

Interrogating which languages carry power disrupts the majoritarian story of English as the dominant language (Mitchell, 2013). The dominance of English and the justification of achievement based on the assumption of English as the language of learning is neglectful of the linguistic funds of knowledge on which non-English dominant students draw in learning. In Washington River High School, newcomers learned that proficiency in English necessarily preceded subject matter learning. Leveraging students' full linguistic repertoires in learning shifts our practices toward equity. Commins and Miramontes (2005) explain that "[s]tudents learning through two languages can be guided in how they can build on, or transfer, what they already know and are learning in one language to be able to extend what they can express in the other" (p. 144). As such, learning through two languages extends multilingual learners into multiple dimensions. Orienting ourselves toward equity requires that we not only disrupt oppressive ideologies, but that we also reconstitute the foundations of our work with students and families with assets-based ideologies (Valenzuela, 1999).

Articulating a vision of democratic equality (Labaree, 1997), one in which all people are afforded the rights and responsibilities of citizenship solely by their humanity, commits us to more equitable schooling practices. A commitment to democratic equality is an ideology as well, and it carries implications for the ways we structure curriculum and the sociocultural practices within school. Additionally, through this lens, we locate the responsibility for educating democratic citizens not just in the school but also in the community.

Ideologies guide the daily life of people in schools. An intentional interrogation of the oppressive ideologies that have structured inequality prompts us to "remake the rules" of the space, rules that were made by others (de Certeau, 1984). As we deliberately reconstruct the space of school undergirded by assets-based ideologies, we shift our orientation toward equity.

Walking Toward Equity: Intentional Practices

As we reconstruct our ways of thinking, we reconstruct our ways of doing. What does it look like to walk toward equity in our daily practices? Drawing on examples from Washington River High School, I offer questions to consider in relation to them—not as a framework or checklist, but rather to invite an exploration of possibilities.

Newcomer students in WRHS experienced duality in their daily lives. For example, many of them were workers and students. They often worked late into the night, and then rose early for school. How might we restructure the school schedule to make space for work? How might we leverage in their learning at school the skills, knowledge, and experiences students learn at work? And, how might we interrogate what knowledge "counts" in order to honor those skills, knowledge, and experiences as learning?

Immigrant students experience the duality of being criminalized and being told that they matter. Backlogs in immigration cases position many immigrants in a liminal space between "legal" and "illegal"—a discursive criminalization of their bodies. How might we reconsider the micro policing of students' bodies and minds that we do in school through dress code policies, cell phone policies, and expectations for behavior? Moreover, how might we interrogate why we surveil students in school at all? Rules certainly have a place in school, but how might we intentionally invite students to participate in constructing the rules by which they live?

Multilingual newcomer students experience the duality of linguistic proficiency (in one or more languages) and linguistic deficiency (in English). While they have developed multilingualism and literacies, their placement in the English Language Learning program and classrooms literally labels them as deficient in English. How might we shift our language to describe their full linguistic repertoire? How might we choose language that is more inclusive of their full biographies? Further, how might we problematize English as the language of learning and leverage all their languages in learning so that content is centered and English is decentered?

When students enter school, they enter a culture of competition—competition for grades, awards, and recognition. An ethos of competition constructs citizens who view one another as adversaries rather than members of the same "public household" (Parker, 2003). What policies and practices of school promote competition? To what end do we foster competition? How might we disrupt these policies and practices to encourage collaboration and support among students?

Overall, WRHS resisted being transformed by the people who walked through its hallways. Are the sociocultural practices inclusive of all students and families? Which languages are used at all? Which ones are used first? What food is served and sold in the cafeteria? How and when are families invited to participate in their students' school experiences? Just as important is the question of how families *are* involved and engaged in their students' school experiences, perhaps in ways not visible or recognized as such by the school. Furthermore, who has access to the announcements, the pep rallies and assemblies, and interactions with all teachers and students?

"Hear Us, See Us" • **107**

Newcomer students in the ELL program at WRHS seldom interacted socially or academically with their general education peers. How might we facilitate authentic interactions between them? How might we leverage these interactions to take up deliberative discussions that allow them to co-construct their daily lives? If we can agree that learning English is necessary cultural capital (Bourdieu & Passeron, 1977) in the United States, how can we ensure that these classes do not serve as a trap?

Finally, newcomers at WRHS constructed citizen identities oriented toward hiding and navigating the margins, and they learned that they were not afforded the rights and responsibilities of citizens. Especially important for newcomers who arrived as high school-aged students is an integrated civic and history education that is mediated by a critical lens so that they see themselves in the narrative of the past, present, and future of the United States. How might social studies curriculum be reconstructed to be more inclusive of multiple perspectives and realities? Who is included in and absent from the stories we tell? How might we critique majoritarian stories and explore counternarratives through curriculum and in the ways in which curriculum is mediated through pedagogy? More importantly, how can students practice democratic skills in the practice of their lives at school?

Disrupting evasion pedagogies that proactively evade opportunities to address equity requires a "[remaking of] the rules" (de Certeau, 1984) of school, and these questions are a start to imagine what better might look like. Creating cultures of belonging means that we are invested in learning from the students, to being what my friend and colleague Aprille Phillips calls *being a student of our students*. Learning from them can teach us how we can walk toward equity in the everyday life of school.

DISRUPTING EVASION PEDAGOGIES IS EVERYONE'S WORK

I entered this classroom with two questions about how students in Washington River High School construct citizen identities: How do high school newcomer students construct citizen identities in social studies? Who are key individuals who influence the construction of citizenship and how do they influence students? This second question lingers for me. In truth, we all are responsible for influencing the construction of citizen identities oriented toward justice and equity. The same is true of disrupting evasion pedagogies; it is everyone's work to advance a "more perfect Union" through the project of teaching and learning.

The students in the ELL classroom at Washington River High School taught me that invisibility has its benefits. While the classroom was a necessary sanctuary, it was also a trap that kept students from participating in the full public realm of school. The challenge for schools and society is to create the conditions in which all citizens are not afraid to be seen and heard, but rather are emboldened to claim space and belonging among "We the People."

REFERENCES

Abedi, J. (2004). The No Child Left Behind Act and English language learners: Assessment and accountability issues. *Educational Researcher, 33*(1), 4–14.

Abrego, L. J., & Gonzales, R. G. (2010). Blocked paths, uncertain futures: The postsecondary education and labor market prospects of undocumented Latino youth. *Journal of Education for Students Placed at Risk, 15*(1/2), 144–157.

Abu El- Haj, T. R. (2007). "I was born here, but my home, it's not here": Educating for democratic citizenship in an era of transnational migration and global conflict. *Harvard Educational Review, 77*(3), 285–316.

Abu El-Haj, T. R. (2009). Becoming citizens in an era of globalization and transnational migration: Re-imagining citizenship as critical practice. *Theory into Practice, 48*(1), 274–282.

Allen, D. (2004). *Talking to strangers: Anxieties of citizenship since* Brown v. Board of Education. University of Chicago Press.

American Immigration Council. (2021, March 16). *The Dream Act: An overview*. American Immigration Council. Retrieved December 28, 2022, from https://www.americanimmigrationcouncil.org/research/dream-act- overview#:~:text=What%20Would%20the%20Dream%20Act,work%2C%20or%20the%20 armed%20services

Antrop-González, R. (2003). This school is my sanctuary: The Dr. Pedro Albizu Campos alternative high school. *Centro Journal, XV*(2), 232–255.

Apple, M. W. (2004). *Ideology and curriculum* (3rd ed.). Routledge.

Apple, M. W. (2014). *Official knowledge: Democratic education in a conservative age* (3rd ed.). Routledge. https://doi.org/10.4324/9780203814383

Learning to Hide: The English Learning Classroom as Sanctuary and Trap
pages 109–118.
Copyright © 2024 by Information Age Publishing
www.infoagepub.com
All rights of reproduction in any form reserved.

110 • LEARNING TO HIDE

Bacon, C. K. (2018). "It's not really my job": A mixed methods framework for language ideologies, monolingualism, and teaching emergent bilingual learners. *Journal of Teacher Education, 71*(2), 172–187.

Bal, A., & Perzigian, A. B. T. (2013). Evidence-based interventions for immigrant students experiencing behavioral and academic problems: A systematic review of the literature. *Education and Treatment of Children, 36*(4), 5–28.

Banks, J. A. (2017). Failed citizenship and transformative civic education. *Educational Researcher, 46*(7), 366–377. DOI: 10.3102/0013189X17726741

Bartolomé, L. I. (2004). Critical pedagogy and teacher education: Radicalizing prospective teachers. *Teacher Education Quarterly, Winter*, 97–122.

Becker, A. (1990). The role of the school in the maintenance and change of ethnic group affiliation. *Human Organization, 49*(1), 48–55.

Bell, D. A. (2009). *Brown v. Board of Education* and the interest convergence dilemma. In E. Taylor, D. Gillborn, & G. Ladson-Billings (Eds.), *Foundations of critical race theory in education.* Routledge.

Bendix, A. (2017, May 17). Immigrant arrests are up, but deportation is down. *The Atlantic.* https://www.theatlantic.com/news/archive/2017/05/under-trump-immigrants-arrests-are-up-but-deportation-is-down/527103/

Bickmore, S., Smagorinsky, P., & O'Donnell-Allen, C. (2005). Tensions between traditions: The role of contexts in learning to teach. *English Education, 38*(1), 23.

Biesta, G. (2004). "Mind the gap!": Communication and the educational relation. In C. Bingham & A. M. Sidorkin (Eds.), *No education without relation* (pp. 11–22). Peter Lang.

Bigelow, M. H. (2010). *Mogadishu on the Mississippi: Language, racialized identity, and education in a new land.* Wiley-Blackwell.

Blitz, L. V., Yull, D., & Clauhs, M. (2016). Bringing sanctuary to school: Assessing school climate as a foundation for culturally responsive trauma-informed approaches for urban schools. *Urban Education, May*, 1–30.

Bloom, S. L. (2005). *Creating sanctuary for children.* Keynote address at the Annual Meeting of the American Association of Children's Residential Centers. Pasadena, CA: October 20, 2005.

Boehm, D. (2016). *Returned: Going and coming in the age of deportation.* University of California Press.

Bogel-Burroughs, N. (2021, March 30). Prosecutors say Derek Chauvin knelt on George Floyd for 9 minutes 29 seconds, longer than initially reported. *New York Times.* https://www.nytimes.com/2021/03/30/us/derek-chauvin-george-floyd-kneel-9-minutes- 29-seconds.html

Boroditsky, L. (2011). How language shapes thought. *Scientific American, 304*(2), 62–65. doi:10.1038/scientificamerican0211-62

Bourdieu, P., & Passeron, J. (1977). *Reproduction in education, society and culture.* Sage.

Boyd, M. (1989). Family and personal networks in international migration: Recent developments and new agendas. *International Migration Review, 23*(3), 638–70.

Bruening, E. (2015). Doing it on their own: The experiences of two Latino English Language Learners in a low-incidence context. In E. T. Hamann, S. Wortham, & E. G. Murillo, Jr., (Eds.), *Revisiting education in the new Latino diaspora.* Information Age Publishing, Inc.

References • **111**

Bush, G. W. (2000, July 10). *George W. Bush's speech to the NAACP's 91ˢᵗ annual convention* [Text]. On Politics. https://www.washingtonpost.com/wp- srv/onpolitics/elections/bushtext071000.htm

Catalano, T. (2017). When children are water: Representations of Central American migrant children in public discourse and implications for educators. *Journal of Latinos and Education, 16*(2), 124–142. DOI: 10.1080/15348431.2016.1205988

Catholic Relief Services. (2010). *Child migration: The detention and repatriation of unaccompanied Central American children from Mexico.* B. Wier, E. Dahl- Bredine, & M. DeLorey.

Cervantes-Soon, C. G. (2014). A critical look at dual language immersion in the new Latin@ diaspora. *Bilingual Research Journal, 37*(1), 64–82.

Chomsky, A. (2007). *"They take our jobs!" And 20 other myths about immigration.* Beacon Press.

Chou, V., & Tozer, S. (2008). What's 'urban' got to do with it? The meanings of 'urban' in urban teacher preparation and development. In F. P. t (Ed.), *Partnering to prepare urban teachers: A call to activism.* (p. 1). Peter Lang.

Commins, N. L., & Miramontes, O. B. (2005). *Linguistic diversity and teaching.* Lawrence Erlbaum Associates, Inc.

Conklin, H. (2008). Modeling compassion in critical, justice-oriented teacher education. *Harvard Educational Review, 78*(4), 652.

Dabach, D. B., Fones, A., Merchant, N. H., & Adekile, A. (2018). Teachers navigating civic education when students are undocumented: Building case knowledge. *Theory & Research in Social Education, 46*(3), 331–373. DOI: 10.1080/00933104.2017.1413470

de Certeau, M. (1984). *The practices of everyday life.* (S. F. Rendall, Trans.). University of California Press.

DeGuzmán, M. (2017). Latinx: ¡Estamos aquí!, or being "Latinx" at UNC-Chapel Hill. *Cultural Dynamics, 29*(3), 214–230.

Deschenes, S., Cuban, L., & Tyack, D. (2001). Mismatch: Historical perspectives on schools and students who don't fit them. *Teachers College Record, 103*(4), 525–547.

Dewey, J. D. (1916 [2011]). *Democracy and education.* Simon & Brown.

Díaz, E., & Deroo, M. R. (2020). Latinxs in contention: A systemic functional linguistic analysis of 11th-grade U.S. history textbooks, *Theory & Research in Social Education, 48*(3), 375–402. DOI: 10.1080/00933104.2020.1731637

Du Bois, W. E. B. (1903). *The souls of black folk: Essays and sketches.* A.C. McClurg and Company.

Dunbar, J. (2012, October 18). *The 'Citizens United' decision and why it matters.* The Center for Public Integrity. https://www.publicintegrity.org/2012/10/18/11527/citizens-united-decision-and-why-it-matters

Duran, E., Gusman, J., & Shefelbine, J. (2005). *Access American history: Building literacy through learning.* Great Source Education Group.

Ernst-Slavit, G., & Wenger, K. J. (2006). Teaching in the margins: The multifaceted work and struggles of bilingual paraeducators. *Anthropology & Education Quarterly, 37*(1), 62–82.

Executive Order No. 13767, C.F.R. 8793 (2017).

Executive Order No. 13769, 3 C.F.R. 8977 (2017).

Fahrenthold, D. A. (2016, October 8). Trump recorded having extremely lewd conversation about women in 2005. *The Washington Post.* https://www.washingtonpost.

112 • LEARNING TO HIDE

com/politics/trump-recorded-having-extremely-lewd-conversation-about-women-in2005/2016/10/07/3b9ce776-8cb4-11e6-bf8a-3d26847eeed4_story.html?utm_term=.e7251fa0806c

Fiorina, M. P., & Abrams, S. J. (2008). Political polarization in the American public. *The Annual Review of Political Science, 11*, 563–588. ·

Flores, W. V. (2003). New citizens, new rights: Undocumented immigrants and Latino cultural citizenship. *Latin American Perspectives, 30*(2), 295–308.

Flores, W. V., & Benmayor, R. (1997). Introduction: Constructing cultural citizenship. In W. V. Flores & R. Benmayor, (Eds.), *Latino cultural citizenship: Claiming identity, space, and rights* (pp. 1–23). Beacon Press.

Fránquiz, M. E., & Salinas, C. S. (2011). Newcomers to the U.S.: Developing historical thinking among Latino immigrant students in a central Texas high school. *Bilingual Research Journal, 34*(1), 58–75.

Freire, P. (1970). *Pedagogy of the oppressed*. Penguin Books.

García, O., & Wei, L. (2014). *Translanguaging: Language, bilingualism and education*. Palgrave Macmillan Pivot.

Gatti, L. (2016). *Toward a framework of resources for learning to teach: Rethinking U.S. teacher preparation*. Palgrave.

Gay, G. (2002). Preparing for culturally responsive teaching. *Journal of Teacher Education, 53*(2), 106–116.

Gentemann, K. M., & Whitehead, T. L. (1983). The cultural broker concept in bicultural education. *The Journal of Negro Education, 52*(2), 118–129.

Gitlin, A., Buendía, E., Crosland, K., & Doumbia, F. (2003). The production of margin and center: Welcoming-unwelcoming of immigrant students. *American Educational Research Journal, 40*(1), 91–122.

Gonzalez, N., Moll, L., & Amanti, C. (2005). *Funds of knowledge: Theorizing practices in households, communities, and classrooms*. Lawrence Erlbaum.

Graham, P. A. (1987). Black teachers: A drastically scarce resource. *Phi Delta Kappan, 68*(8), 598–605.

Gray, T. (2021). "I am their teacher": How a Latina paraeducator 'remakes the rules' of school by being there. In A. Phillips & T. Gray (Eds.), *Agency in constrained academic contexts: Explorations of space in educational anthropology*. Lexington Books.

Grossman, P. L., Hammerness, K., & McDonald, M. (2009). Redefining teaching, re-imagining teacher education. *Teachers and Teaching: Theory and Practice, 15*(2), 273.

Grossman, P., & Loeb, S. (2008). Taking stock: Future directions for practice and research. In P. Grossman, & S. Loeb (Eds.), *Alternative routes to teaching* (p. 187). Harvard Education Press.

Gutiérrez, K., Rymes, B., & Larson, J. (1995). Script, counterscript, and underlife in the classroom: James Brown versus *Brown v. Board of Education. Harvard Educational Review, 65*(3), 445–471.

Gutmann, A. (1987). *Democratic education*. Princeton University Press.

Gutmann, A. (1988, June 5). Moral education in our public schools: We need to teach our children the civic virtues that make democracy work. *The Washington Post*. https://www.washingtonpost.com/archive/opinions/1988/06/05/moral-education-in-our-public-schools/014417be-4769-4da2-933e-3a3f2bfef50c/

References • 113

Hagen Gray, T. M. (2017). *"Hear us, see us": Constructing citizenship in the margins.* [Unpublished doctoral dissertation]. University of Nebraska-Lincoln. Available from https://digitalcommons.unl.edu/dissertations/AAI10682492/

Hamann, E. T. (1995). *Creating bicultural identities: The role of school-based bilingual paraprofessionals in contemporary immigrant accommodation (two Kansas case studies).* [Unpublished Master's thesis]. University of Kansas.

Hamann, E. T. (2002). ¿Un paso adelante? The politics of bilingual education, Latino student accommodation, and school district management in southern Appalachia. In S. Wortham, E. G. Murillo, Jr., & E. T. Hamann (Eds.), *Education in the new Latino diaspora: Policy and the politics of identity.* Ablex Publishing.

Hamann, E. T., & Harklau, L. (2015). Revisiting education in the new Latino diaspora. In E. T. Hamann, S. Wortham, & E. G. Murillo, Jr., (Eds.), *Revisiting education in the new Latino diaspora.* Information Age Publishing, Inc.

Hamann, E. T., & Reeves, J. (2013). Interrupting the professional schism that allows less successful educational practices with ELLs to persist. *Theory Into Practice, 52*(2), 81–88.

Hamann, E. T., Wortham, S., & Murillo, Jr., E. G. (Eds.). (2015). *Revisiting education in the new Latino diaspora.* Information Age Publishing, Inc.

Hamann, E. T., Wortham, S., & Murillo, Jr., E. G. (2002). Education and policy in the new Latino diaspora. In S. Wortham, E. G. Murillo, Jr., & E. T. Hamann (Eds.), *Education in the new Latino diaspora: Policy and the politics of identity.* Ablex Publishing.

Hammerness, K., & Matsko, K. K. (2012). When context has content: A case study of new teacher induction in the University of Chicago's urban teacher education program. *Urban Education, 48*(4), 557–584.

Haneda, M. (2009). Learning about the past and preparing for the future: A longitudinal investigation of a grade 7 'sheltered' social studies class. *Language and Education, 23*(4), 335–352.

Harklau, L., & Colomer, S. (2015). Defined by language: The role of foreign language departments in Latino education in southeastern new diaspora communities. In E. T. Hamann, S. Wortham, & E. G. Murillo, Jr., (Eds.), *Revisiting education in the new Latino diaspora.* Information Age Publishing, Inc.

Haug, S. (2008). Migration networks and migration decision making. *Journal of Ethnic and Migration Studies, 34*(4), 585–605.

Hess, D. E. (2008). Democratic education to reduce the divide. *Social Education, 72*(7), 373–376.

Hess, D. E., & McAvoy, P. (2015). *The political classroom: Evidence and ethics in democratic education.* Routledge.

Hilburn, J. (2014). Challenges facing immigrant students beyond the linguistic domain in a new gateway state. *Urban Review, 46*(1), 654–680.

Hilburn, J., Journell, W., & Buchanan, L. B. (2016). A content analysis of immigration in traditional, new, and non-gateway state standards for U.S. history and civics. *The High School Journal, 99*(3), 234–251. doi:10.1353/hsj.2016.0008

hooks, b. (1994). *Teaching to transgress: Education as the practice of freedom.* Routledge.

Immigration Reform and Control Act (IRCA). (1986). Pub. L. No. 99-603, § 100, Stat. 33-15(1986).

114 • LEARNING TO HIDE

Irizarry, J. G. (2007). Ethnic and urban intersections in the classroom: Latino students, hybrid identities, and culturally responsive pedagogy. *Multicultural Perspectives, 9*(3), 21–28.

Jackson, P. W. (1968). *Life in classrooms.* Teachers College Press.

Jaffe-Walter, R., & Miranda, C. P. (2020). Segregation or sanctuary? Examining the educational possibilities of counterpublics for immigrant English Learners. *Leadership and Policy in Schools, 19*(1), 104–122. DOI: 10.1080/15700763.2020.1714057

Jaffee, A. T. (2016). Social studies pedagogy for Latino/a newcomer youth: Toward a theory of culturally and linguistically relevant citizenship education. *Theory & Research in Social Education, 44*(2), 147–183. DOI: 10.1080/00933104.2016.1171184

Kimmerer, R. (2013). *Braiding sweetgrass: Indigenous wisdom, scientific knowledge and the teachings of plants.* Milkweed Editions.

Kopan, T. (2016, August 31). What Donald Trump has said about Mexico and vice versa. *CNN Politics.* http://www.cnn.com/2016/08/31/politics/donald-trump-mexico-statements/

Labaree, D. F. (1997). Public goods, private goods: The American struggle over educational goals. *American Educational Research Journal, 34*(1), 39–81.

Labaree, D. F. (2010). *Someone has to fail: The zero-sum game of public schooling.* Harvard University Press.

Ladson-Billings, G. (2004). Culture versus citizenship: The challenge of racialized citizenship in the United States. In J. A. Banks, (Ed.), *Diversity and citizenship education* (pp. 99–126). Jossey-Bass.

Ladson-Billings, G., & Tate, W. F. (1995). Toward a critical race theory of education. *Teachers College Record, 97,* 47–68.

Lamphere, L. (1992). Introduction: The shaping of diversity. In L. Lamphere (Ed.), *Structuring diversity: Ethnographic perspectives on the new immigration.* University of Chicago Press.

Lamphere, L., Grenier, G., & Stepick, A. (1994). Introduction. In L. Lamphere, A. Stepick, & G. Grenier (Eds.), *Newcomers in the workplace: Immigrants and the restructuring of the U.S. economy.* Temple University Press.

Lamphere, L., Stepick, A., & Grenier, G. (Eds.). (1994). *Newcomers in the workplace: Immigrants and the restructuring of the U.S. economy.* Temple University Press.

Lau v. Nichols, 414 U.S. 563 (1974)

Leeman, J. (2018). Critical language awareness and Spanish as a heritage language: Challenging The linguistic subordination of US Latinxs. In K. Potowski (Ed.), *Handbook of Spanish as a minority/heritage language* (pp. 345–358). Routledge.

Levine, P. (2007). *The future of democracy: Developing the next generation of American citizens.* University Press of New England.

Levinson, M. (2012). *No citizen left behind.* Harvard University Press.

Liptak, A. (2023, July 1). Along with conservative triumphs, signs of new caution at Supreme Court. *New York Times.* https://www.nytimes.com/2023/07/01/us/supreme-court-liberal-conservative.html

Lomawaima, K. T., & McCarty, T. L. (2002). When tribal sovereignty challenges democracy: American Indian education and the democratic ideal. *American Educational Research Journal, 39*(2), 279–305.

López, G. R., & Velásquez, V. A. (2006). "They don't speak English": Interrogating (racist) ideologies and perceptions of school personnel in a Midwestern state. *International*

Electronic Journal for Leadership in Learning, 10 (29). http://iejll.synergiesprairies. ca/iejll/index.php/ijll/article/view/629/291

Love, B. J. (2004). *Brown* plus 50 counter-storytelling: A critical race theory analysis of the "majoritarian achievement gap" story. *Equity & Excellence in Education, 37*(3), 227–246. https://doi.org/10.1080/10665680490491597

Matias, C. (2016). *Feeling White: Whiteness, emotionality, and education.* Sense Publishers.

McAvoy, P., & Hess, D. (2013). Classroom deliberation in an era of political polarization. *Curriculum Inquiry, 43*(1), 14–47.

Milner, H. R. 2006. The promise of black teachers' success with black students. *Educational Foundations, 20*(3–4), 89–104.

Mitchell, K. (2013). Race, difference, meritocracy, and English: Majoritarian stories in the education of secondary multilingual learners. *Race Ethnicity and Education, 16*(3), 339–364.

Moll, L. C., Amanti, C., Neff, D., & Gonzalez, N. (1992). Funds of knowledge for teaching: Using a qualitative approach to connect homes and classrooms. *Theory Into Practice, 31(2),* 132- 141.

n.a. (2010). *Illegal immigration costs taxpayers.* (Postcard sent from anti-immigration proponents to residents of Washington River leading up to the special election on a controversial city ordinance).

National Council for the Social Studies (NCSS). (2013). *Revitalizing civic learning in our schools.* https://www.socialstudies.org/position-statements/revitalizing-civic-learning-our-schools#fn5

NCSS. (2016). A vision of powerful teaching and learning in the social studies. *Social Education, 80*(3), 180–182.

Nieto, S. (2006, Spring). *Teaching as political work: Learning from courageous and caring teachers.* The Longfellow Lecture conducted at Sarah Lawrence College, Bronxville, NY.

Nieto, S., & Bode, P. (2012). *Affirming diversity: The sociopolitical context of multicultural education* (6th ed.). Pearson.

No Child Left Behind (NCLB) Act. (2001). Pub. L. No. 107-110, § 115, Stat. 1425 (2002).

Noddings, N. (1988). An ethic of caring and its implications for instructional arrangements. *American Journal of Education, 96*(2), 215–230.

Oboler, S. (Ed.). (2006). *Latinos and citizenship: The dilemma of belonging.* Palgrave Macmillan.

Olbermann, K. (2016). 176 reasons Donald Trump shouldn't be president using Trump's own words. *GQ, The Closer.* http://www.gq.com/story/176-reasons-donald-trump-shouldnt-be-president-olbermann

Paris, D., & Alim, H. S. (Eds.). (2017). *Culturally sustaining pedagogies: Teaching and learning for justice in a changing world.* Teachers College Press.

Parker, W. C. (2003). *Teaching democracy: Unity and diversity in public life.* Teachers College Press.

Peralta, C. (2013). Fractured memories, mended lives: The schooling experiences of Latinas/os in rural areas. *Bilingual Research Journal, 36,* 228–243.

Pew Research Center. (2014a, April 10). *The next America.* P. Taylor. http://www.pewresearch.org/next-america/

116 • LEARNING TO HIDE

Pew Research Center. (2014b, July 22). *Children 12 and under are fastest growing group of unaccompanied minors at U.S. border*. J. M. Krogstad, A. Gonzalez-Barrera, & M. H. Lopez. http://www.pewresearch.org/fact-tank/2014/07/22/children-12-and-under-are-fastest-growing-group-of-unaccompanied-minors-at-u-s-border/

Pew Research Center. (2015, March 9). *U.S. immigrant population projected to rise, even as share falls among Hispanics, Asians*. A. Brown. http://www.pewresearch.org/fact-tank/2015/03/09/u-s-immigrant-population-projected-to-rise-even-as-share-falls-among-hispanics-asians/

Phillips, A., & Gray, T. (2021). Introduction: Taking up space in anthropology and education. In A. Phillips & T. Gray (Eds.), *Agency in constrained academic contexts: Explorations of space in educational anthropology*. Lexington Books.

Posner, G. M. (2004). *Analyzing the curriculum* (3rd ed.). McGraw-Hill.

Putnam, R. D. (2000). *Bowling alone: The collapse and revival of American community*. Simon & Schuster Paperbacks.

Reeves, J. R. (2004). "Like everybody else:" Equalizing educational opportunity for English Language Learners. *TESOL Quarterly, 38*(1), 43–66.

Reid, E. (2017, September 25). Eric Reid: Why Colin Kaepernick and I decided to take a knee. *The New York Times*. https://www.nytimes.com/2017/09/25/opinion/colin-kaepernick-football-protests.html

Rodríguez, N. (2015). Teaching about Angel Island through historical empathy and poetry. *Social Studies and the Young Learner, 27*(3), 22–25.

Rosa, J. (2019). *Looking like a language, sounding like a race. Raciolinguistic ideologies and the learning of Latinidad*. Oxford University Press.

Rosaldo, R. (1994). Cultural citizenship and educational democracy. *Cultural Anthropology, 9*(3), 402–411.

Rubin, B. C. (2012). *Making citizens: Transforming civic learning for diverse social studies classrooms*. Routledge.

Russell, S. G., & Mantilla-Blanco, P. (2022). Belonging and not belonging: The case of newcomer students in diverse US schools. *American Journal of Education, 128*(4), 617–645.

Santa Ana, O. (2002). *Brown tide rising: Metaphors of Latinos in contemporary American public discourse*. University of Texas Press.

Sarroub, L. K. (2002). In-betweenness: Religion and conflicting visions of literacy. *Reading Research Quarterly, 37*(2), 130–148.

Scott v. Sanford, 60 U.S. 393 (1856)

Sensoy, O., & DiAngelo, R. (2017). *Is everyone really equal? An introduction to key concepts in social justice education* (2nd ed.). Teachers College Press.

Shalaby, C. (2017). *Troublemakers: Lessons in freedom from young children at school*. The New Press.

Sharma, A., Schmeichel, M., & Wurzburg, E. (2023). Introduction: The twin motors of neoliberalism and progressivism. In A. Sharma, M. Schmeichel, & E. Wurzburg (Eds.) *Progressive neoliberalism in education: Critical perspectives on manifestions and resistance*. Routledge. doi: 10.4324/9781003224013-2

Short, D. (2002). Language learning in a sheltered social studies class. *TESOL Journal 11*(1), 18–24.

References • **117**

Short, D., Echevarría, J., & Richards-Tutor, C. (2011). Research on academic literacy development in sheltered instruction classrooms. *Language Teaching Research, 15*(3), 363–380.

Siham Fernández, J. (2021). *Growing up Latinx: Coming of age in a time of contested citizenship.* NYU Press.

Simpson, L. B. (2017). *As we have always done: Indigenous freedom through radical resistance.* University of Minnesota Press.

Soo Hoo, S. (2004). We change the world by doing nothing. *Teacher Education Quarterly, 31*(1), 199–211.

Spradley, J. P. (1979). *The ethnographic interview.* Holt, Rinehart and Winston.

Spring, J. (2012). *Deculturalization and the struggle for equality* (7th ed.). McGraw Hill Education.

Stull, D. D., Broadway, M. J., & Erickson, K. C. (1992). The price of a good steak: Beef packing and its consequences for Garden City, Kansas. In L. Lamphere (Ed.), *Structuring diversity: Ethnographic perspectives on the new immigration.* University of Chicago Press.

Tollefson, J. W. (1991). *Planning language, planning inequality.* Longman.

United Nations. (1948). *Resolution 217: Universal declaration of human rights.* United Nations General Assembly: Paris, France.

United States Census Bureau. (2010). *Quick facts.* Author. http://quickfacts.census.gov/qfd/states/

United States Department of State. (2017). Honduras 2017 crime & safety report. https://www.osac.gov/Pages/ContentReportDetails.aspx?cid=21167

U.S. Const., amend. XIV, § 1.

Valdés, G. (1996). *Con respeto: Bridging the distances between culturally diverse families and schools.* Teachers College Press.

Valdés, G. (2001). *Learning and not learning English: Latino students in American schools.* Teachers College Press.

Valenzuela, A. (1999). *Subtractive schooling: U.S.-Mexican youth and the politics of caring.* State University of New York Press.

Viesca, K. M., & Gray, T. (2021). Disrupting evasion pedagogies. *Journal of Language, Identity & Education, 20*(3), 213–220. DOI: 10.1080/15348458.2021.1893173

Ware, F. (2006). Warm demander pedagogy: Culturally responsive teaching that supports a culture of achievement for African American students. *Urban Education, 41,* 427–456.

Watson, W., Sealey-Ruiz, Y., & Jackson, I. (2016). Daring to care: the role of culturally relevant care in mentoring Black and Latino male high school students. *Race, Ethnicity and Education, 19*(5), 980–1002.

Wilson, V. (2020). *Inequities exposed: How COVID-19 widened racial inequities in education, health, and the workforce. Testimony before the U.S. House of Representatives Committee on Education and Labor.* 116th Cong. (testimony of Valerie Wilson). https://www.epi.org/publication/covid-19-inequities-wilson-testimony/

Wortham, S., Murillo, Jr., E. G., & Hamann, E. T. (Eds.). (2002). *Education in the new Latino diaspora: Policy and the politics of identity.* Ablex Publishing.

Wright, W. E. (2010). *Foundations for teaching English language learners: Research, theory, policy, and practice.* Caslon Publishing.

Wuthrow, R. (2018). *The left behind: Decline and rage in rural America.* Princeton University Press.

Yosso, T. J. (2005). Whose culture has capital? A critical race theory discussion of community cultural wealth. *Race, Ethnicity, and Education, 8*(1), 69–91.

AUTHOR BIOGRAPHY

Tricia Hagen Gray is Assistant Professor of Practice in the College of Education and Human Sciences at the University of Nebraska-Lincoln. She has also worked as a Postdoctoral Research Associate in the International Consortium for Multilingual Excellence in Education (ICMEE) housed at UNL. Her fifteen years as a high school Spanish teacher in contested spaces—including an urban context, a public school located on Native American tribal lands, and an exurban community experiencing demographic change—inform her work in meaningful ways. Her research questions aim to center and amplify the experiences of marginalized young people to inform more equitable and justice-oriented schooling. She lives in Nebraska with her life partner their two children.

Learning to Hide: The English Learning Classroom as Sanctuary and Trap
page 119.
Copyright © 2024 by Information Age Publishing
www.infoagepub.com
All rights of reproduction in any form reserved.

Printed in the United States
by Baker & Taylor Publisher Services